POLITICAL INSTITUTIONS AND ISSUES IN BRITAIN

Also by James Cable
GUNBOAT DIPLOMACY
THE ROYAL NAVY AND THE SIEGE OF BILBAO
*GUNBOAT DIPLOMACY, 1919–1979 (Second Edition)
*BRITAIN'S NAVAL FUTURE
*DIPLOMACY AT SEA
*THE GENEVA CONFERENCE OF 1954 ON INDOCHINA

As Grant Hugo
BRITAIN IN TOMORROW'S WORLD
APPEARANCE AND REALITY IN INTERNATIONAL RELATIONS

*Also published by Macmillan

Political Institutions and Issues in Britain

James Cable

© Sir James Cable 1987

Softcover reprint of the hardcover 1st edition 1987

All rights reserved. No reproduction, copy or transmission of this publication may be made without written permission.

No paragraph of this publication may be reproduced, copied or transmitted save with written permission or in accordance with the provisions of the Copyright Act 1956 (as amended), or under the terms of any licence permitting limited copying issued by the Copyright Licensing Agency, 33–4 Alfred Place, London WC1E 7DP.

Any person who does any unauthorised act in relation to this publication may be liable to criminal prosecution and civil claims for damages.

First published 1987

Published by
THE MACMILLAN PRESS LTD
Houndmills, Basingstoke, Hampshire RG21 2XS
and London
Companies and representatives
throughout the world

Typeset by Wessex Typesetters
(Division of The Eastern Press Ltd)
Frome, Somerset

British Library Cataloguing in Publication Data
Cable, James, *1920–*
Political institutions and issues in
Britain.
1. Great Britain—Politics and
government—1979–
I. Title
320.941   JN231
ISBN 978-0-333-40541-3   ISBN 978-1-349-18765-2 (eBook)
DOI 10.1007/978-1-349-18765-2

For Viveca, as always

Contents

Preface	ix
1 Introduction	1
2 The Absence of a Written Constitution	12
3 The Executive in Britain	22
4 Legitimacy: Queen, Lords and Commons	33
5 How Cabinet and Commons Operate	45
6 The Servants of the State	56
7 The Rivals of the State	66
8 The Commonwealth	77
9 Parties and Factions	87
10 Divisions on Constitutional Issues	99
11 Divisions on Economic and Social Policy	108
12 Divisions on Foreign and Defence Policy	118
13 The Special Problem of Ulster	129
14 Civil Liberties in Britain	139
15 The Scope for Change	148
Bibliography and Further Reading	159
Index	168

Preface

This book is the outcome of a series of lectures on British Politics delivered to the International Summer School at Cambridge. It owes much to the many questions asked by that cosmopolitan audience and still more to the extensive reading undertaken both before and after that stimulating experience. Otherwise my acquaintance with politics is derived from three and a half decades of direct observation – and of discussion with practising politicians: as an official at home and a diplomat abroad.

Officials are not, of course, supposed to take any active part in British politics, but they cannot do their job (or expect promotion) unless they understand the political system. Diplomats abroad have a harder task. They must not merely know how the political process operates in the country where they are stationed. They must also explain it, briefly and simply, to incredulous ministers at home. The obvious method – equally applicable when explaining British practice to foreigners – is to draw parallels and point to contrasts.

Personal experience has thus inclined me to attempt explanation by comparison: between politics in Britain and abroad; between politics today and in the past. Readers will quickly realise which prejudices have coloured these comparisons, but my bias is personal and not systematic. Objectivity is naturally unattainable by writers on politics. Even if they support no party, they can scarcely avoid belonging to a nation, a class, a sex, a race or an age group. Those who escape the influence of their roots are soon conditioned by education, by experience, by interest.

If the author has his prejudices, readers need not share them. This book is intended to inform, at worst to provoke, not to convert. It is meant to be a simple account, in a single volume, of the British political system as this existed in the later eighties; of the sources of political power and influence in Britain and of the political issues of most concern to the British people. As an academic subject politics has been sliced into as many specialisms as medicine. Mine is a general practitioner's product: aimed at the intelligent reader with enough time – and interest in British politics – for a single book.

With that reader in mind there are no footnotes. In politics all statements are controversial. Instead there is a list of books used and of books offering different opinions. Anyone seriously interested should try some of them. Many have an ideological commitment that will not be found in these pages. Living in various countries under contrasting systems of government is a disillusioning experience.

JAMES CABLE

1 Introduction

The simplest definition of politics is the struggle for power over people. It is a very widespread activity and it does not just take place in national elections or inside the Kremlin or in party caucuses or in all the thousands of much-publicised gatherings that we are accustomed to think of as specifically political. It starts on school playgrounds and it is not unknown in old people's homes. It happens in universities, in churches, in corporations, in hospitals, in tennis-clubs, in the armed forces: in every group, however small, however private, however specialised, which offers to the ambitious a chance to exercise power over people.

Power over people can be an objective as attractive, as compelling, as all-absorbing as sexual satisfaction. Fortunately the urge to power is less widespread than the sexual impulse. Otherwise the human race would have wiped itself out long ago. Many men and women have other interests or else are too lazy, too fastidious or too timid to take part in the struggle for power. Some positively prefer to have things arranged for them, to be told what to do. Others just want to be left alone.

Whenever a group of human beings comes together – whether lastingly because they all live in the same village, or fleetingly because they have been stranded for half a day in the transit lounge of some remote airport – these different human characteristics emerge. Some passively accept or wait. Others want to do something, to organise, to agitate. They often disagree about what should be done. The active argue among themselves, try to convert one another, attempt to mobilise support among the passive. That is politics.

This book is concerned with one particular aspect of politics: the struggle within Britain, and the conventions that are supposed to regulate that struggle for power over the British people, British national politics. This is a broad subject with rather fuzzy boundaries. People can start with much more limited ambitions – power in a town council, in a trade union, in some commercial or industrial enterprise – yet end by seeking to influence the conduct of the state or the destiny of the nation. If they do not, if they are content with a limited sphere of activity, concerned only to mind their own parochial business, then I shall have little to say about them. On the other hand, I shall not confine myself to the doings of ministers, members of parliament or political parties. There are many other people and organisations who influence and seek to influence the conduct of the state and the destiny of the nation, even if it is only by advising or criticising, by carrying out orders or by disobeying them. The authority of any national government depends on the attitudes adopted by this important minority of people involved, one way or another, in national politics.

Their involvement has two main motives exemplified in two questions asked by Lenin, who devoted his entire life to politics and nothing but politics. The first question needs no explanation: What Is To Be Done? But more often he emphasised as the fundamental issue: Who? Whom? Who gave orders to Whom? Whose interests, opinions, decisions were to prevail over Whose opposition?

Lenin, in common with many other politicians whose ideas were otherwise quite different from his, was aiming at supreme power: the widest and strongest authority over the maximum number of people. The great majority of the power-hungry have more limited ambitions. The centurion in the New Testament is a good example. He said:

> I am a man under authority, having soldiers under me; and I say to this man, Go, and he goeth; and to another, Come and he cometh; and to my servant, Do this and he doeth it.

He was a man content to obey orders as long as he could also give them, ready to uphold a political system in which he had a small, but significant stake. That need not have prevented him from intriguing for promotion, nor from taking sides for or against one of the generals whose ambitions so often plunged Roman provinces, even the Empire itself, into turmoil. But most of his modern equivalents, in all walks of life and each of the world's many nations, are more modest. They enjoy and value a limited authority and influence which they do not intend to put at risk by attempting too much, whether for themselves or for the general good. They are content with their relatively humble position as junior members of the governing class and with the system that gives them some privilege.

In every country there is a governing class. The universal system of government is that the majority, who are insufficiently interested in the process to give it their full attention, are ruled by a minority. That minority is the governing class, even if most of them know they have no chance of getting to the top, can at best expect to be advisers or administrators, must usually console themselves with the limited power of passing on to those beneath them, perhaps with a shade of personal interpretation, the orders they have received from above. They are members of the governing class because they have some power over some people. Most of them, of course, hope for more.

'Governing class' is a more convenient expression than 'ruling class', which has confusing overtones. A ruling class may be so defined – whether on the basis of race, parentage, religion, language or, as the Marxists would have it, ownership of the means of production – that it includes many persons neither active nor interested in politics. The existence of such a class may even be regarded as sustaining or justifying or motivating not only the exercise of political power, but the state itself. Those who actually exercise power are merely the agents, conscious or unconscious, of a class greater than they are and with more enduring interests. These are intriguing ideas, but their proper place is in a different kind of book.

A governing class is a simpler and more universal concept. Someone who actually exercises or who might plausibly come to exercise some power over the people of his or her country belongs to the governing class. It does not matter whether he could also be described, as could one British Foreign Secretary, Ernest Bevin, as a member of the working class or, as could one of his successors, Lord Carrington, as a member of the aristocracy. Soldiers too have very different origins and sympathies, but they come to resemble one another, and to be distinguishable from civilians, in more ways than the wearing of uniform. Of course, members of the British governing class are not interchangeable any more than the governing classes of all countries are identical. But the relationship between rulers and ruled does not vary quite as much as all rulers like to pretend.

What most distinguishes one governing class from another is how you get into it; to what checks and restraints the governing class is subject; and how the composition or the objectives of the governing class can be changed.

There is usually some kind of minimum qualification for getting into the governing class. In the Soviet Union, for instance, it is not enough to belong to the Communist Party, though even that is not very easy for most people. Candidates must be proposed by a member in good standing and approved by the local party committee before they can join. Only 10 per cent of the adult population get that far. The ambitious must then achieve entry to the *Nomenklatura*. Broadly defined, this is a list of about 2 million office-holders whose appointment, transfer or promotion requires specific party approval at every stage. These 2 million are about 12 per cent of the Party or a little over 1 per cent of the adult population. Many of them are in rather humble jobs, never get much further and enjoy very little of the power and privilege we associate with a governing class. But at least they have got to the starting-line.

In other countries it may be necessary to belong to a particular tribe, or religious sect or to the Army, to qualify. In Saudi Arabia it used to be essential to be related to the Royal Family – a large group, because of polygamy, but still a small minority. More recently the complications created by oil wealth have made the admission of a few outsiders unavoidable, but the Royal Family is still the core. So it was, in 1984, in Romania, where the top 50 members of the governing class were all related to Nicolae Ceausescu, the Conductor, and the second tier mostly owed their posts to the patronage of members of the ruling family.

In the United States one has to be rich or to become rich.

These are all minimum qualifications. Many of those who qualify never get anywhere near real power, because they lack either the will or the ability or both. There are also always outstanding exceptions. When he started his political career, Adolf Hitler did not seem well qualified to become a member of the German governing class, but he got to the top.

In Britain, ways of getting into the governing class are more various than is often supposed. One of the commonest passports is higher education. Somebody with a university degree stands a better chance of getting into the governing class. Of course, he is more likely to become a university graduate if his parents had enough education themselves to appreciate its value and thus to encourage and support their child in the considerable effort needed to achieve this qualification. Although students in Britain, unlike those in many other countries, have the cost of their fees and maintenance paid from public funds, the academic standards demanded for admission are stiffer and more competitive, so considerable motivation is needed from children still at school. Parental wealth is not a crucial factor (the higher the parental income, the lower is the public grant) but parental education often is. The children of schoolteachers frequently stand a better chance than those from homes with much money but no books.

This is one of several factors which, in Britain as in other countries, impart a hereditary bias to the composition of the governing class. It is even accentuated by the ability of many fee-paying schools to provide a better preparation for university entry than many state schools. Nevertheless, many who achieve great power do so without much education and university graduates are almost as prominent in the Labour Party as they are in the Conservative Party. Education and social origins may influence entry to the governing class: they do not determine it. Nor do they offer a reliable guide to ideological commitment. The best known leader of the Extreme Left in Britain, Tony Benn, inherited a peerage, which he first renounced and has since, in truly Orwellian fashion, attempted to remove from the record of his life, together with his education at Oxford and the private fortune of his American wife. Similarly the British Communist Party has, since 1950, been represented in the House of Lords, but not, avowedly, in the House of Commons.

In Britain, therefore, entry to the governing class does not depend, as it does in the Soviet Union, on acceptance of the received ideas of those already in power. It is not even necessary, as it is in the United States, to profess support for the existing political system. Nor is wealth essential. Naturally, having money helps anyone seeking entry to the governing class by other routes than the Trade Union movement or the parties of the Left. Even so, it is not indispensable and many members of the British governing class acquire money only after they have achieved significant power.

What is more important in Britain than in some countries is apprenticeship in an organisation. Those who aspire to power – in straight politics, in administration, in the armed forces, in the trade unions, even through success in commerce, industry or finance – must usually be prepared to work their way up. The outsider who achieves prominence in national politics in Britain is very much an exception. There is nothing in twentieth-century British history to match the example of General Eisenhower – invited to stand for the Presidency of the United States before he had declared himself as either a Democrat or a Republican. Even switching from one ladder of power to another is much less easy than it is in many European countries. And there are few British examples of people like Dulles or Kissinger – never elected to anything – suddenly finding themselves in positions of tremendous political power.

In Britain membership of the governing class, anywhere near the top, is for professionals: people who have made it their career.

Here are two examples. James Callaghan, Labour Prime Minister from 1976 to 1979, finished his education at 16, became a junior civil servant at 17, joined the appropriate trade union and the Labour Party at 19. At the age of 24 he was a middle-ranking official of his trade union. After war-time service in the Navy he was elected to parliament when he was 33 and, as Labour governments came and went, received ministerial appointments of increasing importance until he became Prime Minister at the age of 64 after 31 years in parliament.

Alec Douglas-Home, Conservative Prime Minister from 1963 to 1964, was educated at Eton and Oxford, elected to parliament at the age of 28, climbed the political ladder and became Prime Minister at the age of 60 after 32 years in parliament. As the eldest son of the 13th Earl of Home he enjoyed all the inherited advantages which Callaghan lacked, but the two of them took much the same time to get to the top and both had to make politics their career.

If we regard the governing class in Britain not as a social or economic class, but as a reservoir of potential governors, one characteristic already briefly mentioned needs to be emphasised: the absence of agreed support for the present political system. Such people as Kinnock, the Leader of the Labour Party and of Her Majesty's Opposition, to say nothing of his more extreme supporters or the leader of the National Union of Mineworkers, Arthur Scargill, must be reckoned as members of the governing class. They exercise power over many people and they might easily come to exercise much more. But they want to change the system – domestic policy, foreign policy, defence policy, even what passes for the British constitution. Their avowed object is to make Britain a different kind of country. Some of them even say they want to introduce *irreversible* change. Of course, such ambitions are often diluted by the actual experience of power, but the sharpness of these ideological divisions needs to be contrasted with the usual picture of the social uniformity of the British governing class. Many of them – in politics, in the civil service, in big business – may share the formative experience of university education, even education at Cambridge or Oxford. But, when this background produces someone with the views of Tony Benn and he has a chance of power, then education, or even social origin, is not enough to foster unity within the governing class. And, if the graduate children of the educated are conspicuous on every ladder that leads to power over people, they are never alone, even on the topmost rungs.

Not everyone, of course, agrees how many people should be counted as belonging to the governing class. Stalin took rather a restrictive view, estimating at 33 000 what he called the 'officers' in the Communist Party of the Soviet Union. Provided we realise that those at the top cannot in practice exercise power over people without the willing cooperation of an extensive hierarchy of subordinates, there is no need to be offensively precise in defining the lower limits of the governing class in Britain. For many purposes the functionary who believes himself to belong to the governing class actually does so. But anyone wholly unconcerned with the government of the country does not belong to the governing class, as that is understood in this book, even if he or she is richer and better known – a comedian, a tennis champion, a pop star – than almost all its members. These are the British equivalents of Russian athletes, ballet dancers, chess champions – famous and highly privileged, but not on the *Nomenklatura*.

The existence within the British governing class of ideological as well as structural differences (Left and Right as well as politician and official or soldier and civilian) encourages competition among different groups to achieve and exercise power over people. This competition is an important influence on the second characteristic earlier suggested as distinguishing the political system of one country from that of another: the extent to which the governing class is subject to constraints in the exercise of power. This is something to be further explored in later chapters, but one aspect is obvious. All governments need both active support from the governing class and the acquiescence of the indifferent majority. A government exposed to organised opposition from the ranks of a divided governing class needs a higher level of popular acquiescence to survive. The risk of losing power is all that prevents most people from abusing power.

It is, of course, through the loss of power or the transfer of power from one group to another that changes occur in the composition or the objectives of a governing class. The way this happens is the third characteristic distinguishing one political system from another, and the nature of the process in Britain will thus have to be more carefully considered later.

Not all changes, however, are large or fast enough for everybody to recognise. When a Democrat succeeds a Republican as President of the United States, the change seems of great importance to American politicians. Most foreigners, however, would find it hard to explain how the replacement of one party by another might alter the composition or objectives of the American governing class. Still greater expertise is needed to distinguish the regime of Brezhnev from that of Andropov, Chernenko or even Gorbachev. Yet, in the Soviet Union as in the United States, fifty years of political evolution, imperceptible at the time as the flow of glaciers, have brought fundamental changes.

British politics are more volatile – something often forgotten by people who see the surprising continuity of British institutions – the monarchy, the procedure of the House of Commons, the University of Cambridge – and who are deceived by these appearances into overlooking the extent and the pace of the real changes in the composition and the objectives of the governing class.

The survival of any organised society usually depends on finding a compromise between two conflicting requirements: change and stability. Change is needed because political aspirations and the economic and technological environment are always altering. Stability is needed because change is inherently disturbing. When too much is changed too fast, people become disorientated and chaos ensues – a frequent aftermath of revolutions. Different societies have found very different kinds of compromise, but one can perhaps distinguish two broad patterns. The first is to start by changing all the appearances so as to reconcile the impatient to a much more gradual transformation of the realities. The other is to preserve the appearances in order to persuade the apprehensive that the pace and extent of real change are tolerable.

In most cases, including even revolutions, the critical appearances are institutions. The French, after the revolution of 1789, swept them all away, even the calendar, but later found it necessary to restore them under different names. After 1917 the Russians did much the same, but in both cases the apparent restoration of institutions masked an enduring change in the composition of the governing class. The Americans, after 1776, changed all the names, but kept most of the institutions and postponed real political change. The British have always preferred to preserve appearances.

In Britain the last two centuries have seen a remarkable continuity in the names and forms of most political institutions. But the governing class has not merely been expanded: its composition has been radically altered and the range and diversity of its political objectives have increased to an extent not always appreciated abroad. Today, for instance, it is still scarcely conceivable that an avowed socialist could become President of the United States, nor can American socialists be regarded as members of the governing class. In Britain there have been eight socialist governments in the last sixty years, but there are still unsatisfied aspirations in this and other directions. Since 1970 the divisions within the governing class have further sharpened. The relative consensus of the fifties and sixties, even of the seventies, has largely disappeared.

The British political system and the British social structure in which I grew up half a century ago may look much the same on paper, but, in many of their practical aspects, are now almost unrecognisable. Reality, in Britain, changes faster than appearance.

When I was a boy, for instance, power over people, for the British governing class, meant power – not always absolute power of course – over about a quarter of the human race. That was the British Empire – the largest the world had ever known. Now British politics is about 50 million islanders in the North Sea. It was not only in Britain that the adjustment of mental processes to the change sometimes proved slow and difficult.

As much might be said of a less momentous change. In the same inter-war period half a century ago, most members of the British governing class could be described, recognisably if not always accurately, as gentlemen, a name then often conceded to anyone whose public school education enabled him to speak standard English with an appropriate accent. Nowadays the word is vanishing, even from lavatory doors.

Naturally these two changes were connected. The maintenance of Empire had been a task that required from even junior members of the governing class the acceptance of responsibility and the exercise of authority. The Empire not only offered more opportunities than would otherwise have been available to those seeking power over people: it conferred on the jobs thus created a prestige that much exceeded their material rewards. This notion that status might be derived from responsibility rather than wealth or talent influenced others besides the servants, actual or aspiring, direct or ancillary, of Empire. In the first few decades of the twentieth century it was a significant element in the ethos of the British middle class and the dominant principle of their educational system: the public (which meant private and fee-paying) schools. These produced gentlemen, of whom a minority maintained the Empire and set the tone for the majority who did not. As the Empire declined and the jobs it had created lost their significance, being a gentleman became less attractive. It is now neither a condition nor even an adequate qualification for entry to a governing class of mixed origins whose preferred slogans are efficiency or commitment rather than responsibility.

If Britain has changed, so, of course, have the world and Britain's place in that ever-changing world. One cannot discuss British politics today without considering the impact of foreign governments and foreign political ideas on the struggle for power within Britain. This country is much less independent than it used to be. The British politician who asks 'What Is To Be Done?' can no longer make a free choice among the possible answers – in foreign affairs or defence policy, but also in economic policy, in matters of internal security, even in measures of social reform. When we come to consider the practical constraints on the liberty of action of the British governing class and of the British governments produced by the struggle for power within that class, we shall have to take particular account of foreign constraints.

Who? Whom? is another question with important international implications. There was a time – in the nineteenth century, even in the twenties of this century – when a British Prime Minister could assume, sometimes with excessive optimism, that he was Who and foreign rulers were Whom. Nowadays the reverse is more often true. Britain is on the defensive, even rather precariously on the defensive.

But there is still another side to these arguments. Politics in Britain may be overshadowed by international politics, but this does not mean that all the options are closed. The early eighties saw the disappearance in Britain of the degree of consensus on domestic policy that obtained in the fifties and sixties. There are already indications that such British consensus as still exists on external policy may prove equally vulnerable in the later eighties. This is another subject for further examination.

Because of the continuing impact of change, no book about British politics can ever be comprehensive, yet clear-cut and up-to-date. The subject might be better tackled in one of those special films devoted to the growth of plants or the life-cycle of a butterfly. There processes imperceptible in nature are so speeded up as to be obvious to the television viewer. A moving picture thus accelerated would be particularly appropriate for modern Britain, where political change tends to be continuous rather than conspicuous. It is much easier to identify and analyse political developments in countries where periodical revolutions introduce striking changes, which are then frozen – to the great, if unintended convenience of the student – until the next upheaval.

In this book – the static picture of a moving subject – it will constantly be necessary, when describing what exists, whether this is the institutional framework or the specific issues now exciting political dispute, to contrast the present with the past. Such comparisons are needed if we are to grasp what changes have already occurred and thus to realise what alterations the immediate future might bring, even to understand some of the oddities of the actual state of affairs. What we must never suppose, in the course of our examination of British politics today, is that we are looking at something which anybody managed to create. Our subject is something which grew, which is still growing.

2 The Absence of a Written Constitution

Napoleon, who had considerable practical experience in such matters, once remarked that constitutions should be short and obscure. His advice came too late for the United States, who adopted their constitution in 1788. Today it is the oldest written constitution in the world. Most other countries also have written constitutions, but many keep on changing them. France, for instance, has had four in the half-century since 1937 – more than the average European country, but not outrageously so.

Britain is supposed to be one of only six countries that have no written constitution, the others being Israel, Libya, New Zealand, Oman and Saudi Arabia. I say supposed, because the general who carries out a *coup d'état* in Africa or Latin America seldom has time to write a constitution before he is overthrown by a major.

There are advantages as well as disadvantages – and both will have to be further discussed – in Britain's lack of a written constitution. To the writer, however, it is thoroughly inconvenient. Only the politically committed or the academically cloistered can afford to be clear and forthright about the British Constitution. Others find themselves constantly and tediously compelled to qualify their assertions that one kind of political act is required or permitted by the constitution and another forbidden or ignored. Because there is no single text (but any number of piecemeal documents) and no person or body whose interpretation of traditional doctrine is universally accepted as authoritative, the constitutional answers to many political questions of practical importance are open to argument. Those who argue, whether they are among the practitioners or the theorists of politics, usually rely on some respected lawyer or scholar to pick out of the great historical rag-bag of statutes and judgements and precedents the bits that are still valid and also relevant.

All too often, however, it seems that for every expert there is an equal and opposite pundit. Not only do the experts sometimes disagree, but their guiding light, the dominant principle of the British Constitution, is no fixed star. This is precedent. What is constitutional is what was done last time the problem arose. Not all precedents,

The Absence of a Written Constitution

however, point in the same direction or prove equally relevant, nor is it impossible for there to arise a problem without a precedent.

There is a famous example of the way in which important elements of the British Constitution have evolved by piling precedent upon precedent. On 1 January 1712 Queen Anne created 12 new peers, so that opposition in the House of Lords should not prevent the conclusion of a peace treaty supported by a majority in the House of Commons. On that occasion the Queen's exercise of her prerogative, on the advice of her Treasurer, Lord Oxford, took the rest of her ministers by surprise. It did not follow any custom or convention: it was a novel royal initiative in an unfamiliar situation.

Nevertheless this precedent was invoked 120 years later. In 1832 a majority in the House of Commons wanted to pass a Reform Bill intended to make rather a small increase in the number of men (there was then no question of women) allowed to take part in the election of members of the House of Commons. Unfortunately the House of Lords could and did block the Bill in the form demanded by the Commons and by public opinion. So the Government, fearing revolution, extracted from King William IV a promise to create as many peers as might be needed to get the Reform Bill through the House of Lords. This episode had two curious features. Lord Grey, the Prime Minister who persuaded the King, himself regarded the creation of 1712 as an unhappy precedent and the King did not actually have to create any peers, because the House of Lords let the Bill through as soon as they learned of the King's promise. But a doubtful precedent had become, by repetition, a pillar of the unwritten constitution.

Eighty years later still there was another dispute between the House of Commons and the House of Lords. First King Edward VII and then King George V were asked to promise the creation of peers (as many as 500 this time) to enable the House of Commons to prevail over the House of Lords. In November 1910, after the Prime Minister, Mr Asquith, had declared his intention of following Lord Grey's example in 1831 and putting his policy to the test of a general election, King George V gave the contingent promise sought from him. Once again the House of Lords yielded and no new peers had to be created.

And we may not yet have heard the last echo of the surprise that began the year of 1712, 'when the Queen drew a list of twelve lords from her pocket.' In 1980 Tony Benn, formerly Lord Stansgate, suggested that a future Labour Government might wish to expedite the abolition of the House of Lords by recommending the creation of enough left wing peers to get the necessary bill through the Upper House.

There was never much logic, as Lord Grey realised as early as 1831, about the invocation of Queen Anne's example to sanction much later measures as remote from her intentions as they were far beyond the likely bounds of her imagination. The justification advanced for such constitutional pretexts was always that, given the necessary minimum of good will, they saved face and made it easier to avoid revolution by yielding or repression by compromising. Fanatics, unfortunately, sometimes preferred, as they may again, the harshness of their own logic.

Naturally the constitution also has its more deliberate components. But the most ambitious of statutes – the Bill of Rights of 1689 or the Act of Settlement of 1701 – is necessarily drafted to meet the needs of a particular situation. What is not repealed or amended tends to lose its force, even its sense, with the passage of time. The remaining, the living portion of the constitution is what happens to meet the political requirements of some later era. And there is no Supreme Court to decide what that should be or to interpret its meaning. The choice has been, and will inevitably be, determined by the balance of political forces at the time.

Of course, even in countries with thoroughly codified constitutions, real conflicts are not resolved by legal arguments or constitutional provisions. In 1861 the United States had to resolve the issues of secession and slavery by civil war; in 1961 Algerian independence drove French generals into rebellion against their own government. It is in the more frequent minor disputes – the American Watergate Crisis of 1973, for instance – that loyalty to a written constitution may be decisive.

There is nothing precise or permanent about the British Constitution. It is a set of constantly changing assumptions about the nature of the State, the balance of powers within the State and the scope for permissible change. Today those assumptions have three main sources: legislation, precedent and the politician's instinctive sense of what he can get away with. The last is the most important but also the most elusive.

The absence of a written constitution is particularly significant when it comes to legislation. Many countries have sought to entrench their constitutions by requiring special procedures for any amendment or any action by executive or legislature that might encroach on the provisions of the constitution. In Finland, for instance, such measures

The Absence of a Written Constitution 15

may need the support of two-thirds or even five-sixths of the parliament. In the United States the Supreme Court can declare a law passed in the customary manner to be unconstitutional. A bare majority in the British House of Commons can do what it likes, subject only to the delaying powers of the House of Lords (to be discussed later) and to a Royal Veto last exercised in 1707. Of course, successive parliaments have over the centuries passed a great many laws which have had the effect of significantly altering what, at any given time, was customarily regarded as being the constitution. In my lifetime, for instance, laws have been passed to give women the vote; to lower the voting age; to alter, more than once, the rules entitling people to British nationality; to restrict the powers of the House of Lords; to confer legal immunity on foreign, but not British, soldiers in this country; to impose on British subjects the regulations of the European Economic Community. The British Constitution is no longer what I was taught it was when I was at school. But all this has been piecemeal legislation. There has been no considered or comprehensive amendment to the constitution. And the laws, even the most fundamental laws, narrowly passed by one parliament can be easily repealed by the next.

Precedent has been just as important as legislation. The Royal Veto, for instance, has never been legally abolished. From 1910 to 1914 the idea that King George V might veto either the Parliament Bill or the Irish Home Rule Bill was seriously suggested by leading Conservative politicians and certain constitutional pundits. It was even mentioned in discussion between the King and the Liberal Prime Minister, Asquith. It was the fact that this veto had not been used since 1707 that enabled the Prime Minister to stick to the position he had declared in 1910: the Royal Veto was as dead as Queen Anne. Similar, though rather less venerable arguments apply to the present Queen's right to dismiss her ministers, to dissolve parliament against their wishes or to reject their advice to dissolve it. So much time has elapsed since these powers were last employed in Britain (though there are recent Australian and Canadian instances) that their use today might seem shocking.

In 1953 an eminent authority argued that the only important power remaining to the Monarch was that of choosing a Prime Minister when there were rival candidates for the post within the party commanding a majority in the House of Commons. The present Queen did just that in 1957 and 1963 when Conservative Prime Ministers resigned, leaving the succession in dispute. Yet precedent is no more immutable than legislation. After 1963 the Conservatives followed the example set by

Labour and started electing a new leader as soon as there was a vacancy and seemed thereby, in practice rather than in principle, to have deprived the Queen of her discretionary power. Before this change could acquire the sanctity of a precedent, the pattern of the political kaleidoscope shifted. The Alliance of the Liberals and Social Democrats made sufficient progress in popular esteem to suggest that a general election might produce a House of Commons in which no party had a clear majority.

In September 1985 the leaders of the two political parties – the Liberals and the Social Democrats – most likely to profit from such a contingency initiated a discussion of its constitutional implications. Although David Steel and David Owen agreed in their identification of the key issue as being the criteria which should constitutionally guide the Queen in choosing someone to form a government and in deciding to grant or refuse an early dissolution of parliament, the views they expressed to their respective party conferences were otherwise dissimilar. The Conservative and Labour parties did not immediately commit themselves to any opinion, though some leading members of the Labour Party may be said to have provoked the discussion by their earlier rejection of the idea that one outcome of a hung parliament might be a coalition government. The views expressed by the Editor of *The Times* and the learned correspondents whose letters he published were no less diverse. Whether or not, as the *Observer* confidently reported at the time, the Queen's Private Secretary really had asked the Secretary of the Cabinet to consult the experts and produce a memorandum on the subject, the absence of general agreement on this aspect of the constitution was obvious. Yet it is easy to imagine circumstances in which the political character of the next government could depend on the view taken by the Queen of her constitutional obligations.

One of the reasons why reliance on precedent makes uncertainty an inevitable element of the British Constitution is that it is not always easy to be sure that a precedent has won sufficient acceptance to become established. When Lord Home was appointed Foreign Secretary in 1960, there was an outcry from the Labour Party that this was unconstitutional because, for twenty years, successive Foreign Secretaries had always been in the House of Commons. Yet Mrs Thatcher chose another peer, Lord Carrington, as Foreign Secretary in 1979. It was also on her advice that the Queen, in 1983, created a couple of hereditary peers, a prerogative supposed by some to have lapsed, because it had not been exercised for twenty years. For over eighty years no Prime Minister has come from the House of Lords and, since King George V chose Mr Baldwin rather than Lord Curzon in 1923, it has been generally supposed that precedent requires a Prime Minister to sit in the House of Commons. But can we be sure? Until 1979 the unbroken precedent of two and a half centuries required the Prime Minister to be a man.

Precedent, moreover, is always less important than what politicians think they can get away with in the circumstances of the time. The true deterrent to the exercise of many royal powers still in theoretical existence has always been the thought of the potential consequences. If the Monarch, say, were to dismiss a government and order a general election, the absence of recent precedents might be forgiven if the election produced a resounding majority prepared to endorse the Monarch's action. But would it? And would that majority last long enough to prevent the constitutional impartiality of the Sovereign being called in question? What would be the ultimate consequences for the very survival of the Monarchy? Of course, in some extreme and unlikely case these risks might be worth running: to prevent the establishment of a totalitarian regime, for instance.

Again, in the Second World War, legislation was passed to extend the life of the House of Commons, to suspend traditional liberties and to assume extraordinary powers over citizens and their property. In that desperate situation what would otherwise have been considered unconstitutional measures went through without significant opposition. It would not happen in normal times or in an emergency that divided rather than united the nation.

For centuries, moreover, the institutions of the established State – Monarch, Lords, Commons, administration and judiciary – have had to take account of the irregular manifestations of popular sentiment. In 1794 Pitt's government, frightened into a witch-hunt by the French Revolution, charged a dozen men with high treason for advocating 'representative government', but, after successive juries had acquitted the first three, abandoned the remaining prosecutions. Lord Grey, whose Reform Bill took a bold stride towards representative government in 1832, attended the first trial, that of the shoemaker Hardy, and thought he would himself have been prosecuted if the jury's verdict had gone the other way.

In February 1985 another jury acquitted a civil servant named Ponting of a lesser offence under the Official Secrets Act because they disapproved of the law as the judge had interpreted it in exhorting them to find him guilty. That law will probably have to be changed as the penal laws of the early nineteenth century were changed when juries refused to convict on capital charges of petty theft.

There are limitations, much more potent than any written constitution could impose, on the powers of any British monarch, government or parliament. These limitations are created by popular feeling, by the ability of ordinary people, particularly when organised, to disobey even lawful commands, by the balance of real political power in the country.

If Britain's unwritten constitution is sometimes confusingly uncertain, it is also flexible. That proved useful in 1975. Until that year most people would have argued that a national referendum or plebiscite, though often employed in other countries, was an expedient unknown to the British Constitution. The one exception, the plebiscite of March 1973, in which an absolute majority of the people of Northern Ireland voted to stay in the United Kingdom rather than join the Republic of Ireland, was both regional and, because it related to Ulster, regarded as one of those exceptions which prove no rules. Because they had so often helped to sustain the rules of foreign dictators, plebiscites were even regarded in Britain with actual distrust.

In 1975, however, exceptional measures were needed to heal the deep divisions within the Labour Party on the issue of British membership of the European Economic Community, which Britain had joined in 1972 under the Conservative government of Edward Heath. The Labour Prime Minister, Harold Wilson, favoured staying in, as did some of his senior colleagues and a minority of Labour members of parliament. But the Party Conference had pronounced for withdrawal. Renegotiating the terms of British participation, allowing members of the Cabinet publicly to express divergent views, obtaining a handsome majority (thanks to Conservative votes) in the House of Commons did not suffice to reconcile Wilson's conception of the national interest with the need for party unity. A national referendum was accordingly held on 5 June 1975 and produced a 2-1 majority in favour of continued Community membership. Although even today some of the Community's Labour critics remain of the same opinion still, the referendum did achieve, as perhaps nothing else could have, Wilson's twin objectives of keeping Britain in the Community and the Labour government in power.

At the time the Conservatives opposed the principle of a referendum, though Margaret Thatcher did concede in 1977 that the device might have its uses in certain labour disputes. But it was again a

The Absence of a Written Constitution 19

Labour government, under James Callaghan, who were the next to employ it. Once more exceptional circumstances called for a flexible approach.

In the sixties the Scottish National Party, hitherto a small and almost insignificant group advocating independence for Scotland, at last succeeded in electing some members of parliament. By February 1974 they had 7 members in a House of Commons where the Labour government needed votes from minor parties to maintain their precarious majority and stay in power. The general election of October 1974 somewhat increased the Labour majority, but the number of Scottish Nationalists rose to 11.

Long before the parliamentary situation became acute a Royal Commission had been appointed in 1969 to consider possible methods of devolving certain powers from the central government in London to regional authorities or assemblies in Scotland and Wales (where an even smaller independence party was active). The issue had excited even greater interest than could normally have been expected because of the discovery of important oil deposits in the North Sea and the contention of the Scottish Nationalists that these should be the exclusive property of an independent Scotland. Even those opposed to independence were deeply divided on the issue of devolution between those regarding it as an acceptable substitute and those fearing it would only prove the first step on a long and slippery path.

The Labour government thus had mixed motives for producing two elaborate and complicated bills, which pleased very few people in England or beyond, providing for limited devolution, legislative rather than executive, in both Scotland and Wales. To get them through (both bills were enacted in 1978) each had to provide for automatic repeal unless endorsed by separate referendums in Scotland and Wales. A late amendment required at least 40 per cent of the electorate in Scotland (but not in Wales) to vote 'yes' to avoid automatic repeal.

A referendum was indeed held in Scotland – and another in Wales – on 1 March 1979. Scotland voted by 32 per cent to 30 per cent in favour of devolution, Wales decisively against. The outcome did not save the government, which was defeated by one vote in the House of Commons on 28 March, resigned and lost the ensuing general election, but it did preserve the unity of the United Kingdom. The Scottish National Party obtained only 2 seats in the elections of 1979 and 1983. Scottish nationalism is no longer important in British politics. The fundamental issue – one of the most serious that can confront any nation-state – of the right to secession had been successfully defused by a constitutional innovation for which there were only two precedents in British history. The respite will not necessarily be permanent. That it was achieved at all was one of the advantages derived from the flexibility conferred by the absence of a written constitution. Consider once again how different was the outcome in the United States in 1861.

Admittedly this remarkable constitutional precedent has its disquieting aspects. The innovation of a referendum was chosen in 1974 (when the prospect was foreshadowed in the Labour Party's electoral manifesto) and repeated in 1979 primarily to serve the interests of a particular political party, to ensure that they retained that power over people which is the supreme objective of all political parties. If these precedents are invoked in future, the purpose of the next referendum may not be as respectable, nor the outcome as satisfactory, as even a Scot may concede to have been the case in 1975 and 1979. Most constitutional expedients, old or new, can naturally be abused as well as used.

The British Constitution, to be further explored in its practical applications in the chapters that follow on British institutions, is not written, so it cannot be precisely and simply described. There is no Supreme Court or other impartial organ able to provide an interpretation of the constitution that would be legally binding on all concerned.

At any given time, therefore, different leaders can honestly take different views of the nature of the constitution and of which actions would or would not be constitutional. In normal times and on minor issues there is usually a sufficient consensus of opinion. But when disagreement sharpens into conflict, political considerations, not legal arguments, determine which of the conflicting views will prevail.

Uncertainty is increased because the constitution is changing all the time, as new laws are passed, as fresh precedents are created, as generally accepted ideas of what you can get away with undergo a continuous process of evolution.

The disadvantages of this peculiar political system are that it is untidy, hard to understand, uncertain and provides inadequate legal restraints on rash innovation or the conduct of the struggle for political power.

The advantages are that it is more flexible, easier to adapt to changing circumstances, less prone to premature obsolescence than systems codified by a written constitution.

It also suits the British temperament, which distrusts theory, logic and lawyers, preferring improvisation to planning. The favourite slogan of the British governing class is that every problem should be treated on its own merits.

Nobody who thinks of the British Constitution as a machine – something created by a rational engineer – a motor car, say, with an engine and a steering wheel, gears and brakes – will ever understand it.

The British Constitution is a living organism. Every day some of its cells are dying and others are being born or transforming themselves into new shapes or functions. The biologist who studies it can never complete his description because the organism has changed while he is still making his notes. All he can attempt – all I shall try to do – is to distinguish the characteristics that are now dominant from those that are merely emerging or are already recessive.

3 The Executive in Britain

The effective source of authority in Britain today is Her Majesty's Government, otherwise known as The Government or The Cabinet: twenty-odd Ministers (the exact number varies) headed by the Prime Minister. Most of them are also heads of major government departments: Foreign Office, Home Office, Treasury and the like. A few of them may (again the practice varies) have no specific departmental responsibilities, but are included in the Cabinet either to manage business in the House of Commons or the House of Lords or simply because their political influence makes their advice worth having. The Cabinet has a collective authority and its members are free to express their views and exert their influence within the Cabinet on any subject, whether or not it is one for which they have specific departmental responsibility. They have a confusing variety of titles, many of them archaic, which may or may not have some particular significance. The Chancellor of the Exchequer, for instance, is always responsible for finance and the Lord Chancellor for the judiciary, but the Lord Privy Seal or the Lord President of the Council may have any kind of job. These two, unlike the Lord Chancellor, do not even have to be lords. Most of the Cabinet are called either Secretary of State or Minister for this or that. But they are all of them members of the Cabinet and all of them must also be members of either the House of Lords or the House of Commons.

The Cabinet has more political power than anyone else. Collectively the Cabinet can issue orders to a whole hierarchy of subordinate ministers, known as ministers of cabinet rank, ministers of state and parliamentary under-secretaries, all of whom must also be members of one or other house of parliament. Then there are the separate, but also subordinate, hierarchies of the permanent civil service, the armed forces and a rich variety of other national officials and organisations. The Cabinet control the entire administration of the country.

They also initiate nearly all legislation and determine most of the agenda for the House of Commons. Collectively or individually they decide most senior appointments and promotions – in the civil service, the armed forces, the judiciary, the Church of England (but not the Church of Scotland or any other churches) – and they exercise a wide-ranging, but not exclusive, power of patronage in the police, the nationalised industries and elsewhere. Because the numerous, separately elected and theoretically autonomous local government authorities of Britain are nowadays heavily dependent for their day to day functioning on subsidies from central government, the Cabinet can also exert powerful influence on them. The Cabinet concentrates and centralises the executive authority of the State.

Unfortunately, as always in the British political system, there are elements of ambiguity and uncertainty in this authority. It is, for instance, debatable whether the authority of the Cabinet is truly collective or whether all its members are subordinate to a superior power vested in the Prime Minister personally. Again, it is clear in constitutional theory that the Cabinet enjoys no intrinsic authority – only that delegated by either the Crown or Parliament – but the application in practice of this principle is sometimes less obvious.

The individual authority of the Prime Minister is certainly considerable. Constitutionally there are many powers which the Prime Minister can exercise on his or her own and without consulting, let alone securing the agreement of, the Cabinet. The Prime Minister can resign and recommend to the Sovereign either the choice of another Prime Minister or the dissolution of Parliament and new elections. If he does either, the rest of the Cabinet lose their positions as well, unless they are reappointed by the new Prime Minister. The Prime Minister can call on a member of the Cabinet to resign and advise the Monarch to appoint a successor. Either power may be used or threatened to over-ride opposition within the Cabinet. Macmillan, when Prime Minister, replaced almost a third of his Cabinet at one go in 1962. A Prime Minister enjoys all the characteristic advantages of a chairman over the agenda, priorities, discussions and recorded conclusions of the Cabinet. Many powers of patronage are his rather than those of the Cabinet – from the appointment of ministers to that of bishops or of the Master of Trinity College at Cambridge.

In 1963 Richard Crossman, a writer and journalist of some distinction who was also an experienced politician, argued forcefully that the ascendancy of the Prime Minister had become so great as to make him the Chief Executive. Other Cabinet Ministers had become mere subordinates or advisers to the Prime Minister.

Crossman supported this view (which he put forward before he himself became a Cabinet Minister) with numerous arguments. As much as a third of the majority party in the House of Commons might hold ministerial posts of some kind. They held them during the pleasure of the Prime Minister, who had appointed them and it was on his continued favour, rather than that of the Cabinet, that their hopes of early promotion depended. With the confidence fostered by this essentially personal support, Prime Ministers often felt able to take important decisions in consultation with only a handful of their colleagues, either in some committee of the Cabinet or even in private. Such business was sometimes not even revealed to the full Cabinet before it became public knowledge, in which event the doctrine of the collective responsibility of the Cabinet required Ministers to defend decisions taken without their knowledge or participation.

There have been many such cases, notably: Anglo-French staff talks before the First World War; the decision to build a British atomic bomb after the Second World War; the conduct of the Suez adventure in 1956 or of the Falklands War in 1982. Even in the discharge of their routine duties, British officials are often aware of secrets which they are allowed to discuss with only certain Ministers.

Prime Ministers, including Margaret Thatcher, can and do over-rule departmental Ministers or dismiss them. By the end of August 1986, 16 members had left Mrs Thatcher's Cabinet, few of them of their own free will.

Even Ministers with no cause to fear such extreme measures hesitate to put forward their proposals without first ascertaining (through their Private Secretaries) that no objection need be feared from the Prime Minister. Mrs Thatcher is not the first holder of her office capable of frightening some of those supposed to be her colleagues in the Cabinet. The old concept of a Prime Minister as no more than the first among equals, the Chairman of the Cabinet, no longer holds good.

But it would still be wrong to suppose that he or she enjoys the autocratic powers constitutionally vested in the President of the United States or of France. Nor have developments since 1963 borne out Crossman's prediction that the ascendancy of the Prime Minister was bound to go on increasing.

Curiously enough, some of the most striking exceptions to what might be called the Crossman Law (though others have advanced similar arguments) have been provided by his own party, the Labour Party. In 1969, for instance, opposition in the Cabinet forced the Prime Minister to drop a plan, to which he had committed himself, to introduce legislation on industrial disputes. In 1974 Harold Wilson, again Prime Minister, not merely failed to impose on a divided Cabinet his policy on the European Economic Community, but had to make an unusual departure from constitutional precedent: the long-established doctrine of the collective responsibility of the Cabinet was suspended and individual Ministers allowed to express opposing views in parliament and the country. Although Tony Benn has complained of 'The Absolute Premiership', he himself was a Minister whom premiers could neither discipline nor dismiss. Moreover, the Labour Party in parliament, when in opposition, nowadays elect some of their members to form a so-called Shadow Cabinet. This is likely to act as a growing constraint on the ability of a Labour Premier to make a free choice of his Ministers and will thus impair his powers of patronage. As he himself must be chosen – and periodically confirmed – as Party Leader by a conference including representatives of the trade unions and constituency parties, he might even be displaced from office by a majority outside parliament.

These tendencies have not yet prevailed in the Conservative Party, where Margaret Thatcher seems to enjoy even more ascendancy than many of her predecessors. From time to time, however, the media report her as having had to yield when her proposals encountered opposition in the Cabinet. And, as happened with former Prime Ministers, Conservative or other, she has found it politically expedient to consider the views of the Party when choosing Ministers and to keep some of whom she would personally rather be rid.

Lord Wilson, himself an ex-Prime Minister of considerable experience, has maintained that no recent Prime Minister has been either a puppet or a puppet-master; that the Prime Minister has more power than any individual Minister, but not more than a Cabinet united against him. Of course, the ability of the Cabinet to restrain the Prime Minister varies from one government to another and is much influenced by the personalities of those concerned and by the balance of real political power they represent. Bearing in mind that a future Prime Minister might have to preside over a coalition government, which past experience suggests as a particularly difficult task, it is hard to be sure which way change is most likely to go. So far, however, the collective authority of the Cabinet is not dead nor is the Prime Minister yet an autocrat.

In the past this has been important. In 1953, for instance, the Prime Minister was Winston Churchill, who enjoyed exceptional personal prestige and ascendancy. When he suffered a major stroke, the Cabinet carried on without him for two months. When that happened to President Woodrow Wilson, the government of the United States was exercised by Mrs Wilson, the only person, except for doctors and nurses, allowed into the President's bedroom, from which she would emerge to declare that the President had agreed to one proposal or had rejected another. In 1954 a group of British Cabinet Ministers agreed that Churchill, who had never fully recovered from his stroke but was still Prime Minister, should not be allowed to attend a summit meeting with the Russians, because he was not fit to conduct negotiations. It is uncertain who in the United States could take a similar decision if President Reagan suffered a stroke. Churchill, after all, did not admit his own incapacity.

Whatever the precise balance of power, now or in the future, between Prime Minister and Cabinet, neither can claim a direct right to this authority. Prime Ministers are not elected by the nation in the way in which American or French Presidents are. A Prime Minister is appointed by the Queen because he commands a majority in the House of Commons, which usually means that he is also the leader of the party with most seats in the House of Commons. I say usually, because in a coalition government the Prime Minister has not always belonged to the largest party.

To describe the authority of the Prime Minister as being derived and indirect is not mere formalism. It is a political as well as a constitutional reality. It is the media who are in error when, in their anxiety to personalise every issue, they represent a general election as a contest between two or more individual leaders, one of whom is then chosen as Prime Minister by a popular vote. There are two main arguments against this view.

One is the widely held opinion that voters are more influenced by party loyalties, by the record of the last government and by the programmes put forward than by personalities. This is naturally hard to prove and necessarily varies from one election to another. The classical example is the decisive rejection by the voters in 1945 of the famous and popular Winston Churchill in favour, not of Attlee personally, but of the Labour Party and the prospect of change. In 1979 the Conservatives won the election, although Mrs Thatcher was less experienced, less well known and probably less popular than James Callaghan. The 1983 election was lost by Labour even more than it was won by the Conservatives, but the voters were rejecting the Labour Party, with its internal dissensions and extravagant proposals, and not just the hapless Michael Foot.

The second argument is more conclusive. Even if a Prime Minister can claim that the result of an election demonstrated a degree of popular personal support, that may not apply to a successor. Churchill became Prime Minister in 1951 as a result of a general election; Eden was merely appointed to succeed him when Churchill resigned. The same happened to Macmillan when Eden resigned and to Callaghan when Wilson resigned. All those Prime Ministers subsequently fought a general election, but two of them lost it. Yet, in principle and in practice alike, they were just as fully Prime Minister during the period (years in the case of Macmillan and Callaghan) before their claim to the post was submitted to the judgement of the electorate.

So a politician does not need a general election to become Prime Minister and even after a successful election it is at least uncertain whether people voted for the person or the party. And the composition of the Cabinet has never been made the subject of a popular vote.

Prime Ministers thus derive their authority from three sources: appointment by the Monarch; the support of a majority in the House of Commons; and selection by their political party. So do Cabinets, but they do not receive their authority directly, only at the instance of the Prime Minister, though this might change in a future Labour government. How authority is obtained from these three sources and the relative importance of each will be considered in the next chapter, but we must first examine the nature of the powers thus delegated to the Executive.

The idea of the Monarch conferring power may seem surprising. We are accustomed to hearing that the Queen reigns, but does not rule and, as an individual, the Queen does indeed enjoy very little power. But the powers of the Crown, which the Queen embodies, are considerable, although they can be exercised, both in constitutional theory and in practice, only on the advice of ministers. Ambassadors, for instance, are appointed by the Queen, whose representatives they are. So is the Foreign Secretary, whose full title is Her Majesty's Principal Secretary of State for Foreign Affairs. Officers of the armed forces and of the Diplomatic Service receive their commissions from the Queen.

This may seem only a formality. The names of prospective ambassadors, once chosen by the Foreign Secretary, sometimes in consultation with the Prime Minister, are submitted for the Queen's approval before their appointment can be confirmed, but Her present Majesty, unlike some of her predecessors, is not known to have objected to any of these proposals. To appreciate the significance of the British procedure this must be compared with the practice in the United States. There the President, who is not only Chief Executive but Head of State, must submit his nominations of ambassadors, cabinet ministers and a host of other important functionaries, military and civil, to the Senate for approval. That process is by no means a mere formality. On the contrary, it adds considerably to the gaiety of nations when unkind cross-examination reveals some unfortunate ambassador as being unable to put a name to the capital or the prime minister of the country for which he is destined. Not all presidential nominations survive this remorseless scrutiny.

There is no such hurdle to pass in Britain. In the splendid words still employed today:

> Whereas it appears to Us, Elizabeth the Second by the Grace of God etc. etc. expedient to nominate some Person of approved Wisdom, Loyalty, Diligence and Circumspection to represent Us . . . We do appoint him.

The Queen signs at the top, the Foreign Secretary at the bottom. That is the Royal Prerogative, nowadays exercised by Ministers, but without specific parliamentary approval. The appointment of ambassadors is one of its less important applications.

Millions of people, for instance, hold British passports without ever realising that they have no legal right to them. Passports – originally permits to leave the kingdom – are issued in the exercise of the Royal Prerogative.

The extent today of the Royal Prerogative, which is in practice largely the prerogative of Ministers, is difficult to define with a precision that would command general agreement. When Bagehot, in his classic *English Constitution*, listed all the things Queen Victoria could do without the consent of parliament – from dismissing the entire army to ceding Cornwall to a foreign power – he intended to amuse rather than to instruct. Today even constitutional lawyers have to admit that the Royal Prerogative comprises all those traditional powers which parliament has never got round to abolishing or restricting. Provided, of course, that they are exercised on the advice of Ministers and do not conflict with political realities.

In foreign affairs, for instance, the prerogative gives British Ministers a wider discretion than that enjoyed by the President of the United States. But no sensible government would stand on their constitutional rights and declare war, make peace or conclude a major treaty without giving the House of Commons a chance to express their views. But treaties are still ratified by the Queen on the advice of Ministers, the only concession to parliament being that the text of the treaty is laid on the table of the House of Commons for 21 days beforehand. And the day-to-day conduct of British foreign policy does not have to be endorsed by parliament or even disclosed to parliament. Although the prerogative is most prominent in foreign affairs, it has many other applications. By its means parliaments are dissolved or summoned, elections held, judges appointed, various executive decisions given legal effect. A frequent expedient is the Order in Council. This is an order by the Queen, whether on the basis of an act of parliament conferring discretionary powers on the executive or in the exercise of the prerogative, which is issued on the advice of Her Privy Council.

The Privy Council is a remarkable body. Anyone who becomes a Cabinet Minister is created a Privy Counsellor for life. But so are many other distinguished people, for whom membership is primarily a high distinction, carrying the title of Right Honourable and entailing little obligation other than a special oath of loyalty and secrecy. The full Council, about 390 strong, meets only on the death of the Sovereign or the announcement of His or Her intention to marry. There is never any question of a vote and normal business is transacted by a handful of members (3 is a quorum) who must always have the consent of the Minister responsible. He signs the Order in Council 'By Her Majesty's Command' and if parliament were ever to object to the arbitrary fist of executive power within this traditional glove, it is he who would be held responsible.

Because parliament, if they choose, can override the prerogative, they provide Ministers with a more important authority. This may take the form of an act of parliament which Ministers have themselves caused to be drafted and have persuaded parliament to pass. More often it is an act passed by an earlier parliament and under a different government, which has remained in force because it has never been repealed. Sometimes this produces odd situations. More than one Labour government, for instance, has exercised emergency powers, which their own supporters would not have granted them, under an act passed by an earlier government against Labour opposition.

Not all acts of parliament, of course, remain in force until they are repealed. The bulk of the government's expenditure and the various forms of taxation which finance it are only authorised by parliament for a year at a time. Various other acts of parliament are deliberately given a time limit when they are passed. Until 1957 the Army Act, which permitted the maintenance of an army and of military discipline, had to be passed afresh every year – a survival of the traditional hostility to a standing army which the Crown might use against parliament itself. Even today, by virtue of the Armed Forces Act of 1981, the Army Act, the Air Force Act and the Naval Discipline Act have to be extended annually by an Order in Council approved by both houses of parliament. And, every five years, they must all be re-enacted.

Beside relying on acts of parliament, new or old, for their legal authority, the Cabinet must also look to parliament for their political authority. In certain circumstances an adverse vote in the House of Commons could force the Cabinet to resign: for instance, if the House of Commons refused to pass the budget or rejected some major proposal to which the Cabinet attached great importance. Not every defeat in the House of Commons leads to the resignation of the government (defeat in the Lords has not had this result since 1909). Sometimes the Cabinet withdraw or modify the proposals the House found objectionable. Occasionally the threat of resignation or of calling a general election induces the House to change their mind.

Every government, of course, tries to avoid being defeated in the House of Commons, because any defeat impairs the prestige of the government and weakens its political authority, but, as so often in the British political system, the outcome depends on circumstances and not on any fixed rule. In the famous debate of May 1940, which probably did as much as any parliamentary debate in this century to determine Britain's destiny, the vote of censure on the Chamberlain government was actually defeated by a substantial majority, but Chamberlain resigned because 90 members of his own party had refused to support him.

There is also a more positive aspect to the political authority a government can derive from parliament. When a government encounters strong opposition in the country, has to apply an unpopular policy or suffers some setback in foreign policy or even in war, that government will often ask the House of Commons for a vote of confidence to sustain and fortify its authority. If defeated on a vote of confidence they had themselves demanded, Ministers would normally resign, but otherwise they have a certain discretion to decide for themselves whether or not to treat an adverse note as one of no confidence. This does not, of course, prevent opposition members from shouting 'Resign!' 'Resign!' every time a government is defeated, even on some small or technical issue or when only a small number of members are present on either side.

Finally, both Prime Minister and Cabinet derive some of their power from the political party that supports them. In 1940 and again in 1975 it was not enough for the government that a majority of the House of Commons had voted in their favour. First Chamberlain, then Wilson, also wanted full party backing, though Wilson was clever enough to get it by means of a referendum. In more trivial instances, the Conservative government had to drop proposals about student grants in 1984 when Conservative members revolted and, in July 1985, Mrs Thatcher was alleged by *The Times* to have threatened resignation to deter Conservative members from voting with Labour against pay rises for officials already highly paid.

Party influence, however, is not exerted only in parliament. Ministers of any complexion are exposed to pressure from their party conferences, but Labour are particularly vulnerable because of the powers which the party constitution gives to the conference to elect the party leader and to recommend policies. Moreover, Labour depends on the trade unions, not only for votes in the conference, but for money. 'The Party will never stand for that' is a phrase often heard from the lips of Labour Ministers. Even a Conservative government, which can normally expect greater deference from its own supporters, cannot presume too far on their loyalty or risk alienating the company directors who back them with money or the newspaper editors and proprietors who furnish them with favourable publicity. Eden was perhaps the Conservative Prime Minister most sensitive to any criticism in the press, but only Balfour, in this century at least, paid it no attention.

Finally, most Ministers sit in the House of Commons, want to retain their seats at the next election and, to this end, must rely not only on the support of their party as a whole, but on that of the party organisation in their own constituency. Once again, Labour Ministers are most at risk because of the procedure whereby constituency parties periodically consider whether or not to continue their support for the member who has hitherto represented that constituency in the House of Commons. More than one ex-Minister has been dropped because the policies he supported while in office subsequently incurred the disapproval of the party activists in his own constituency. Conservatives seldom suffer for their loyalty to a former Conservative government, unless there has been a sharp change of course, as from Chamberlain to Churchill.

But Ministers of any complexion may need the special and positive support of their party if they lose their seats at the next election. That has not happened to a Prime Minister since MacDonald in 1935, but lesser ministers have fallen as thickly as autumn leaves. If their careers are not to be seriously interrupted, even ended, by this setback, they have to be found another seat to contest. Sometimes, if the general election returned their party to power, the Prime Minister may create a vacancy by conferring a peerage on a sitting member, but more often the ex-Minister must beg his way from one constituency expecting a by-election to another.

It is, of course, under a coalition government that the need to maintain party support is most capable of dividing Ministers from one another and from the Prime Minister. That was why Curzon, Baldwin and others abandoned their Conservative colleagues in the coalition government headed by Lloyd George and encouraged the party revolt that brought down the Cabinet in 1922.

In Britain, therefore, the Executive is the Cabinet, dominated but not entirely controlled by the Prime Minister. This executive is not directly elected and has no intrinsic legitimacy, but derives its authority and its powers, in unequal proportions, from Crown, Parliament and Party. Of these three the Crown legally confers substantial powers, but can not, in the person of the Monarch, effectively restrict their exercise. Parliament confers greater powers, both in theory and in practice. Parliament also enjoys over the government a power which is real, but seldom used, being held in check by the ability of the Prime Minister to threaten the House of Commons with dissolution and a general election. Legally, Parties can neither give power nor control it, but in practice they are taking a growing share in both functions, particularly in the case of the Labour Party.

4 Legitimacy: Queen, Lords and Commons

Curiously enough, the Queen derives her authority from an act of parliament. In 1701 the Act of Settlement decided that after the death of Queen Anne the Crown should pass to the descendants of Sophia, Electress Dowager of Hanover. It was as the only available Protestant grandchild of King James I and VI that the Electress Sophia was politically so attractive. For another act of parliament, also still in force, had declared that the Sovereign could only be a Protestant and could only marry a Protestant.

It is on the Act of Settlement that the present Queen's right to the throne depends. Of course Her Majesty can trace her descent from Alfred the Great, but so can many other people. In terms of pure genealogy there are rival claimants, at home and abroad, to the least attenuated strain of Tudor or Stuart blood. None of this matters. Parliament decided that only the descendants of the Electress Sophia was eligible and there the Queen's claim is supreme.

It is worth remembering, incidentally, that British monarchs from George I to William IV were also Kings of Hanover, which involved the British in many eighteenth-century wars and might have exposed them to more in the nineteenth century if Hanover had not been lost to the Crown in 1837, because the Salic Law prevented Queen Victoria from succeeding to the Hanoverian throne. But the Channel Islands and the Isle of Man are still Crown dependencies, not part of the United Kingdom or legally subject to the Parliament at Westminster, but with their own legislative assemblies, local administration and separate laws. The Channel Islanders even like to argue that they are only subject to the Queen in her capacity as Duke of Normandy, but they accept the ultimate authority of the Privy Council. The position of other Commonwealth countries of which the Queen is still Sovereign is sufficiently complicated to be reserved for a later chapter.

It is in the United Kingdom of Great Britain and Northern Ireland that the authority conferred on the Cabinet by the Queen owes its legitimacy to her hereditary descent, through the particular ramifications approved by earlier parliaments, from the earliest King of All England, Egbert, who died in the year 839.

In the last quarter of the twentieth century hereditary descent might not be accepted as a legitimate source of authority, if it had not become an important ingredient of one royal function not yet discussed: the Queen's role in what Bagehot called the dignified part of government. Of course, even republican Heads of State can be dignified: nobody was more so than President de Gaulle. Even he, however, was incapable of appealing to so wide a range of human sentiments as a monarch. Nor are his special personal qualifications shared by most republican Heads of State. Usually they are either active politicians – and thus controversial figures, even partisans – or retired politicians and thus a trifle shop-soiled.

A monarch is a more convincing magnet for patriotism as the enduring and inoffensive personification of the nation-state. It is also more natural for human beings to feel loyalty to a person than to a system or a constitution. Even such acutely controversial leaders as Hitler or Pétain commanded greater fidelity than the Weimar Constitution or the Third Republic.

When the monarch can supplement dignity, impartiality and relative permanence by the engaging interest aroused as the head of a conspicuous family, by the glamour of the natural leader of society, by the respectability of setting a moral example and by that special aura of magic and mystery still associated with inherited royalty, there is the potential for a mass appeal beyond the reach of more humdrum Heads of State.

These factors are actually more important today than they were when Bagehot published his book in 1867. To begin with, his chapter on the Monarchy, though still worth reading today, was then already out of date. Queen Victoria's frantic grief at the death of the Prince Consort in 1861 plunged her into a long period of seclusion in which she ceased to perform her more glamorous functions. This was very unpopular and the royal lapse was not redeemed by the Prince of Wales, who may have led society, but not in an elevating manner. The 1870s and 1880s were perhaps the only period in the nineteenth and twentieth centuries in which republicanism was a significant, if still a minority element in British politics.

Fortunately Queen Victoria recovered much ground in her last years, King Edward VII behaved far better as Sovereign than he had as Prince of Wales and both King George V and King George VI were models of all a constitutional monarch should be. They gave the institution such respectability and prestige that it easily survived the brief but unfortunate interlude of the reign of King Edward VIII.

Queen Elizabeth II has given the British monarchy a popularity more general and widespread than it has enjoyed since the reign of Queen Elizabeth I. Although the sense of mass involvement in the activities of Royalty has naturally been the work of the media, particularly television, it goes without saying that increased exposure is of advantage only to those able to stand it. If the magic has grown beneath the Klieg lights and the zoom lenses and in the face of constant intrusion and harassment, it must have been real magic.

When Bagehot remarked that although 'no feeling could seem more childish than the enthusiasm of the English at the marriage of the Prince of Wales' (in 1863) even he might have been surprised at the confirmation, in 1981, of his conclusion: 'A princely marriage is the brilliant edition of a universal fact and, as such, it rivets mankind.' The main difference produced by the passage of almost 120 years was that enthusiasm was no longer confined to the English.

It is more than a coincidence that this increase in the dignified importance of the British monarchy has been matched by a decline in its real political power. Under the influence of the Prince Consort, who was able, intelligent and energetic, though never popular, Queen Victoria had been gradually clawing back some of the royal powers lost, not through legislation but by the precedents the idleness and incapacity of her predecessors had created. One of his last acts, for instance, was to avert a war with the United States by insisting, in the Queen's name, on the amendment of an angry despatch from the Foreign Secretary after the United States Navy had forcibly removed passengers from a British ship on the high seas. But for his premature death there is no telling how far the recovery of royal power might have gone or what the results could have been. As so often before and since, the evolution of the British constitution was altered by accident.

For instance, the rule that important Foreign Office despatches had to be submitted in draft to the Sovereign before being sent abroad was still in force in the reign of King George V (1910–1936). It might not have survived increasing reliance on the telegraph and even the telephone for the conduct of diplomacy, but its abandonment seems to have been the result of another accident. During his brief reign in 1936 King Edward VIII was so careless of his official duties and so slack about reading or looking after the documents sent to him, that the Foreign Office decided they could no longer afford to send him papers that were urgent or secret. Although his successors were meticulous in these respects, a precedent had been created and important instructions from the Foreign Office have subsequently gone to the Sovereign for information rather than even formal approval.

For a variety of reasons, moreover, Queen Victoria's successors have decreasingly imitated her practice, which continued even after the death of the Prince Consort, of vigorously and occasionally even publicly expressing the Royal view on the major political issues of the day. Her interventions were often shrewd and sensible, but the inconvenience and even embarrassment they caused to her Ministers did not increase her popularity in political circles. It was then that republican sentiments were sometimes uttered even within the governing class. Today their expression is generally regarded as electorally suicidal. Although popular acceptance of the mystique of monarchy should not be exaggerated, it is still a factor in the calculations of conventional politicians and a potential reinforcement of those surviving rights of the Queen, as originally defined by Bagehot; to be consulted, to encourage and to warn.

The political developments of recent years have also, as mentioned in Chapter 2, excited renewed interest in aspects of the royal prerogative that had earlier been coming to be regarded as little more than formalities: choosing a prime minister and dissolving parliament. The general election of February 1974 produced a House of Commons in which no party had a clear majority (Labour 301, Conservatives 297, Liberals 14, Others 23). Edward Heath, the Conservative Prime Minister, spent the weekend seeking the support of the Liberal Party to help him remain in office, failed and resigned on the afternoon of Monday 4 March. The Queen then sent for Harold Wilson, leader of the Labour Party. He formed a government which, though in a minority, survived the opening debate on the Queen's Speech (which is, of course, written by the Cabinet to present their own programme to the House of Commons) because the Conservatives abstained in the vote that followed.

Wilson had earlier hinted that, if defeated, he would seek a dissolution. This probably influenced the Conservative decision to abstain, but Wilson later wrote in his book *Final Term*: 'Neither Mr Heath nor I had, or could have had, any idea what the Sovereign's response would have been to so quick a request for a second election.'

In 1979, therefore, Lord Wilson, who was three times Prime Minister, clearly took the view that the Queen could, in March 1974, have refused a request from him for a dissolution, even though the existing House of Commons scarcely offered any obvious third option if Heath's failure to muster a majority had then been followed by Wilson's defeat.

The next general election, however, might open a wider field for

Legitimacy: Queen, Lords and Commons 37

choice within the House of Commons: three parties differing in size, but of the same order of magnitude. In 1923, for instance, the figures were: Conservative 258, Liberal 159, Labour 191. David Butler has explored a range of different combinations and their potential consequences in *Governing Without A Majority*. Here a single scenario will suffice to illustrate the scope for the royal prerogative.

The Alliance win enough seats to offer a secure majority (something the Liberals could not do in March 1974) to either a Conservative or a Labour government on conditions – proportional representation, ministerial participation, even a change in leadership – which the larger parties are reluctant to accept. Each might rather form a minority government of their own if assured of a dissolution as soon as defeated.

The outcome would naturally be determined by many considerations. These would probably include not only the influence of the Sovereign (as in the formation of the National Government in 1931) but also the response expected from the Queen to a request for dissolution. The assumptions which politicians made about the circumstances in which dissolution would be either granted or refused could not fail, from the very outset of post-electoral discussions, to influence their preference for either a coalition or a minority government.

The precedents are somewhat ambiguous. No Prime Minister – and Margaret Thatcher would remain Prime Minister, as did Edward Heath in 1974, until she resigned – has been refused a dissolution this century. In 1916, however, Bonar Law, the leader of the Conservative Party, when invited by King George V to form a government after the resignation of Asquith, the Liberal Prime Minister, sought to make his acceptance conditional on a promise of dissolution, which the King refused. The outcome was a coalition headed by neither the outgoing Prime Minister nor the Leader of the Opposition.

A similar situation could conceivably arise if Mrs Thatcher were to resign after a general election had produced a House of Commons in which no party had a majority. It is arguable that the precedent set by King George V would have to be followed to ensure that all concerned, and not just the existing leaders of the Conservative and Labour parties, were given the chance to muster a majority.

The possibility that such scope might exist for the exercise of the royal prerogative is naturally as repugnant to revolutionary politicians as the mystique of monarchy. To them any alternative – enlisting former Speakers or Prime Ministers, for instance – is preferable. That such proposals have emanated from more conventional quarters is evidence of a failure to understand the necessary basis for the retention of monarchy. Much though the Sovereign has gained by withdrawing from routine political controversy, the elements of magic and mystery might not survive the formal renunciation of the last vestiges of real power. A very little substance is enough to sustain the symbolism of tradition and ceremony, but there must be some if the Sovereign's discharge of the dignified duties of Head of State is to have any meaning and its present added value. The British are too old to play with dolls.

The paradox of esteem for the monarchy rising in step with, perhaps because of, its progressive loss of ordinary political power does not apply to the House of Lords, which survives only because politicians cannot agree how to get rid of it. As early as 1911 the Parliament Act had proclaimed the intention to substitute for the House of Lords 'a Second Chamber constituted on a popular instead of a hereditary basis.'

Three quarters of a century later the House of Lords has approximately 1200 members, of whom nearly 900 are hereditary peers. Only a minority are there because they are bishops or hold high judicial appointments or because some recent government has selected them as life peers. Of course, this minority tend to be disproportionately active in conducting the business of the House of Lords, many hereditary peers being more than content with the privileged position their titles still give them in British and – dare it be said – international society. Nevertheless the House of Lords is still a Second Chamber dominated by the hereditary principle.

This anomaly has survived for three reasons. First, the powers of the House of Lords have been progressively limited to that of delaying non-financial bills passed by the House of Commons – money bills are exempt – for about 13 months. Secondly, many people consider it useful that legislation proposed by the House of Commons should be scrutinised and tidied up in the House of Lords. But the third reason is the most conclusive. It has proved easy to limit the powers of the House of Lords because its composition – whether hereditary or nominated – has lacked legitimacy, on contemporary political assumptions. But, if this archaic House of Lords were to be replaced by a modern Second Chamber elected on some respectably democratic basis, would it be possible to deny to this new body something approaching the powers enjoyed by the Senate of the United States or Second Chambers in other countries? The very idea

Legitimacy: Queen, Lords and Commons

has generally been abhorrent to British politicians reared in the House of Commons.

Although the left wing of the Labour Party would be happy to sweep away the House of Lords without replacing it, other would-be reformers have often shrunk from this extreme step. Would it, they wonder, be sensible to leave no obstacle, however fragile, to the legal ability of a narrow majority in the House of Commons to transform the British constitution, the character of the State and the nature of British society? That once potent antidote to rash legislation – the formula '*La Reyne s'avisera*' – has not been employed since Queen Anne vetoed the Scotch Militia Act in 1707.

No satisfactory answer ever having emerged to these perplexing questions, the British have fallen back on their usual illogical compromise and an obsolete House of Lords survives because a modern Second Chamber might be more effective.

Meanwhile the House of Lords confers no significant legitimacy or authority on the Cabinet. A government does not need a majority in the House of Lords to take office and no Labour government has ever been assured of one. In opposition Conservatives find some merit in the amending and delaying powers of the House of Lords; in office, even Conservatives are quick to remind Their Lordships that these powers must be exercised with caution if they are to survive.

On the whole caution is observed. When governments, Conservative as well as Labour, are defeated in the House of Lords, (on 104 occasions from 1979 to 1986) it is usually on some measure unlikely to survive a second transit through the Commons. That happened in July 1985 to a curious proposal that some children should be caned at school, but that others should be immune. In June 1986, however, the Thatcher government declared their intention of reversing in the House of Commons the amendments passed by the House of Lords to the Social Security Bill.

The chances of the Lords ever stepping forward in the grander role of defenders of the Constitution – for instance, against a Bill to abolish elections and make the House of Commons self-perpetuating – depend on the rather unlikely assumption that anyone intent on revolutionary aims would nevertheless remain anxious to follow legal forms. In other circumstances the attitude of the Upper House would probably have less impact on the country at large than would resistance by the Monarch. The House of Lords enjoys less prestige, being widely regarded as a kind of asylum for inherited privilege and superannuated politicians, a prejudice Peers have recently tried to overcome by having their proceedings televised – a bold experiment which the House of Commons preferred not to risk.

The House of Commons is a different and rather confusing kettle of fish. By virtue of previous legislation, by precedent and convention, because its members are directly elected, it is the supreme source of legitimacy and authority for the Executive. No government can come into existence, nor long survive, without the support of a majority in the House of Commons. Even the powers exercised under the royal prerogative may be challenged by such a majority, no laws may be passed without its consent and there is no restriction on the laws which such a majority can pass or repeal. In the last resort the refusal of supply – which means refusal to authorise the collection of taxes – can reduce any government to legal impotence.

All this is fine in theory, but some practical questions must be asked. Does the House of Commons really reflect the opinions of the people or is its composition distorted by the electoral system and the influence of political parties? Does a majority in the House of Commons really exercise effective control over the government or can it be cowed by the Prime Minister's right to call another election that would put at risk the seat and consequently the power, privileges and salary of every member? Can most members of the House of Commons exercise any independent judgement under the pressure applied by their own party organisation? To use Bagehot's words, is the House of Commons still an efficient or merely a dignified part of the British Constitution?

These are questions often argued today and they will have to be further considered in later chapters about British political parties and the issues that divide them. The short answers that follow may serve to carry the debate forward: they are not generally acceptable conclusions.

The claim that the House of Commons represents the opinions of the British people, for instance, certainly seems doubtful, but not all politicians would admit the arguments against it. These are partly statistical. In 1979, perhaps the most significant recent general election, because it produced a major shift in power and policy, there were three main parties: Conservative, Labour and Liberal. It took nearly ten times as many votes to elect a Liberal member of parliament as it did to elect a Conservative or Labour member. The Liberals got 13.8 per cent of the votes cast and only 1.7 per cent of the seats in the House of Commons. In 1983 the Alliance of the Liberal and Social Democratic parties got 25 per cent of the votes and 3 per cent of the seats. From 1945 onwards no political party has based its majority, sometimes its large majority, in the House of Commons on as much as 50 per cent of the votes cast in a general election. In 1951 the Conservatives got fewer votes than the Labour Party, but more members of parliament; in February 1974 it was the turn of the Labour Party to get more seats with less votes.

All these anomalies spring from the British electoral system. This requires the members of the House of Commons (who are called Members of Parliament) to be chosen in a general election at least once every five years, though special measures were taken, because of the Second World War, to prolong until 1945 the life of the House of Commons elected in 1935. Prime Ministers can, however, and usually do, themselves call general elections at more frequent intervals. When individual members of the House of Commons die or resign, a by-election is held in the constituency concerned to choose a replacement.

The country is divided into 650 constituencies (the number fixed in 1983), each of which elects one member of parliament. Constituencies are all supposed to contain roughly the same number of voters, but have, even in this century, been as large as 218 000 or as small as 11 000 electors. A more usual range is between 35 000 and 100 000. These differences reflect the accidents of geography and population density as well as the tendency of people to move around faster than the Boundary Commission can redraw the constituency map. In each constituency the candidate with the largest number of votes wins the seat. It makes no difference whether he passed his nearest rival by 10 votes or by 10 thousand; whether he had an absolute majority or whether this was the combined achievement of two or more other candidates. The winner takes all and votes for anyone else are wasted.

The system favours parties, such as the Conservatives and Labour, whose support is geographically concentrated rather than evenly dispersed across the country. Now that there is significant backing, at least as displayed in opinion polls and at by-elections, for the Alliance of the Liberal and Social Democratic parties, proposals for changing the system have become a serious issue in British politics and will later have to be considered as such. For the moment we may simply note that the representative character of the House of Commons is open to dispute. Not only is the expression of popular opinion distorted by the electoral system: it is further constrained by the operations of political parties.

In principle, of course, all British subjects and Irish citizens resident in the United Kingdom (except peers, felons and persons convicted of electoral corruption) are entitled, if 18 or over and registered as electors, to vote by secret ballot in a general election at least once every five years. Between 72 per cent and 84 per cent of the electorate do voluntarily exercise this right. If over 21 and with further exceptions (bankrupts, for instance, lunatics, judges and some clergymen and office-holders) they may also present themselves as candidates for election to the House of Commons. There are no primary elections of the kind held in the United States to choose candidates.

But, except in Northern Ireland and parts of Scotland and Wales, any candidate without the backing of either the Conservative, the Labour, the Liberal or the Social Democratic party is almost certain to lose and likely also to forfeit his deposit (formerly £150, now £500) for failing to get a minimum proportion (formerly one-eighth, now one-twentieth) of the votes cast in the constituency. The elector who wants his vote to be effective thus has a restricted choice and, even within this narrow range, where he lives may determine which preference he can express with any hope of significance.

Of course, it can be, and often is, argued that representative democracy cannot function unless popular opinions are canalised in some such manner. This is probably true, but the extent of these constraints should be remembered when weighing the legitimacy of the House of Commons. Its members, after all, were chosen in two stages, of which we have so far considered only the second. Before a serious candidate can even present himself to the electors, he must be chosen by his party. The methods vary and, as this is now a controversial issue, will be further discussed later. Broadly speaking, the choice is made by a committee of members of the particular party in the constituency concerned. Under 4 per cent of the British people ever join any political party and very few of those go to the trouble of getting themselves elected to such a committee. Less than a hundred people may thus be involved in choosing a candidate for a constituency with 80 000 voters.

Such involvement is one way of demonstrating membership of the governing class. It can be quite significant. Many constituencies are regarded by either the Conservative or the Labour party as safe seats, in which party endorsement is enough to ensure election. As many as 200 candidates may seek to be considered for one such seat. Even constituencies regarded as volatile or hopeless may attract many applicants, for contesting an election is one way of acquiring the name and political reputation which may later appeal to the selection committee of a less hopeless seat. Of course, a committee with strong ideological views may prefer a candidate who shares them, even if he is otherwise a relative beginner. The process of selection which every serious parliamentary candidate must undergo before he confronts the electors can vary greatly and is often arbitrary.

Although it is convenient, as well as conventional, to regard the existence of a majority in the House of Commons as an expression of popular preferences, this is one of those pious fictions necessary for the maintenance of orderly government. Its representative character is at best a rough approximation.

It is nevertheless this majority that is the prime source of the government's authority. But, having once conferred authority, can the majority control its exercise? Since at least 1945 this has often been considered doubtful. The growing ascendancy of the Prime Minister in everyday business has given a new persuasiveness to his or her patronage and to the possession of the ultimate weapon: calling a general election. As was the case with the supposed dominance over the Cabinet, the Prime Minister's command over supporters in the Commons, though impressive, has probably been exaggerated by some commentators.

There was always a flaw in the argument about the Prime Minister's power to dissolve a difficult parliament. This is a 'nuclear deterrent': if the threat must be implemented, then the threat has not achieved its purpose. Nor can it be credibly threatened on every occasion or in most circumstances. Dissolution is a final sanction that can reinforce, but not replace, the ordinary constraints of party discipline. These bonds have not, as used to be predicted, become progressively tighter. In the seventies, perhaps because failure in government strained the unity and weakened the popular support of both the major parties, there was even some loss of grip. Between 1972 and 1979, as Norton (1982) has pointed out, governments were defeated in the House of Commons on 65 occasions, something that had not happened so often in the previous hundred years.

In 1979 there occurred a setback that was even more unusual. The Prime Minister, James Callaghan, resigned and recommended the dissolution of parliament, not by his own free and tactical choice, but because his government had been defeated in a vote of confidence on 28 March. Ramsay MacDonald, in 1924, was the only other twentieth-century Prime Minister to be voted out of office by the House of Commons.

Margaret Thatcher's subsequent ascendancy, with larger majorities and more confident leadership, might suggest that the experience of the seventies was exceptional. Yet she, too, has had her setbacks, losing the Shops Bill in April 1986 and being twice defeated in the following July over the secretarial allowances of members. A more severe test will come if a coalition government confronts a House of Commons more evenly divided among more than two parties.

Government supporters in the House of Commons do not continue to vote for the government only because they agree with its policies or out of party loyalty or from the hope of themselves achieving office or being otherwise rewarded. They must also consider their prospects of returning to the House of Commons after the next general election. Members of Parliament have always been privileged enough for most of them to be reluctant to lose that status, once acquired, but to many of them the salary, the allowances, the perquisites and the pension are now of personal economic importance.

But, to be re-elected no less than to be elected for the first time, one must have the support of one's party. The success achieved by Dick Taverne was exceptional, and in recent years unique. In 1972, as a Member of Parliament and ex-Minister, he resigned from the Labour Party, but managed to be re-elected on his own, both in a by-election and in the first of the two general elections in 1974. But that was the end of it.

Even a politician enjoying such a remarkable personal reputation and appeal as Enoch Powell had to seek another party base in Northern Ireland when he abandoned the Conservatives. Those Labour politicians who achieved re-election, as did David Owen, as Social Democrats were much out-numbered by those for whom leaving the Party meant saying goodbye to Parliament.

The ability of the majority in the House of Commons to control the Executive, no less than the freedom of members to exercise their independent judgement, may thus be as open to question as the validity of the concept of representative democracy. Yet none of these ideas is altogether devoid of practical influence. The House of Commons does have some power, even if this is collective and potential and seldom demonstrated in the kind of confrontation that is sufficiently dramatic to correspond in convincing fashion to the models created by the traditions of past centuries. The House of Commons may be only the assembly of the governing class, but this does not diminish its importance. Even the fact that so many people want to join it adds something to the legitimacy of the House of Commons and to its ability at least to influence the exercise of the authority it confers on the Executive.

5 How Cabinet and Commons Operate

To understand how the British political system functions and how it differs from those in other countries, one must first forget about the doctrine of the separation of powers. This idea that the State had three distinct branches – Executive, Legislature and Judiciary – was the result of a misunderstanding by certain French writers, notably Montesquieu, of the British constitution as it existed in the eighteenth century. What these writers should have seen was the usual untidy English muddle of precedent, improvisation and compromise. What they described had been rationalised by their own more logical minds.

In Britain today Executive, Legislature and Judiciary are closely intertwined. Every member of the Cabinet, as earlier mentioned, must also belong to either the House of Lords or the House of Commons. When Macmillan wanted a businessman, or Wilson a trade union leader, in the Cabinet, the outsider had to be given a peerage or got into the House of Commons at a by-election. Ministerial membership is real membership. In some countries ministers may originally be drawn from the parliament, but, once they enter the government, their places in the legislative chamber are taken by substitutes, so that the ministers can concentrate on governing and allow a parliament unfettered by responsibility to get on with legislating.

In Britain, ministers may nowadays spend less time in the House of Commons than did Stanley Baldwin in the twenties and thirties. He was accused of neglecting his duties as Prime Minister to listen to debates. But, while Parliament is sitting, most ministers will be frequent attenders: answering questions, opening or closing debates, voting or waiting to vote, exerting their influence on individual members in the dining-room, the tea-room or the smoking-room. They have offices in the House as well as in their own Departments and officials soon become accustomed to doing business while their minister awaits the summons to vote and even more accustomed to hanging about until he returns. Even the Cabinet must sometimes meet in the Prime Minister's room at the House of Commons.

The duty of voting can be a burden when the government of the day has a narrow majority. In February 1972, the Foreign Secretary, Sir Alec Douglas-Home had to be recalled from an official visit to Tokyo to vote in the House of Commons, an imposition he had escaped while a peer. The House of Lords, incidentally, has the Lord Chancellor as its chairman. Unlike the Speaker of the House of Commons, who is elected by the members of that assembly, the Lord Chancellor is appointed by the Prime Minister. He is also a member of the Cabinet; he is the head of the judiciary, choosing both judges and magistrates; he presides, whenever he wishes, over the handful of judges in the House of Lords, the so-called Law Lords, who constitute the supreme court of appeal in Britain. So much for the separation of powers.

Members of the Cabinet operate in three ways: collectively, in groups and as individuals.

The whole Cabinet normally meet at 10 Downing Street at least once a week. The Prime Minister presides; there is an agenda; conclusions are reached, recorded by the secretariat and circulated to those who need to know. As anyone who studies the minutes – called Cabinet Conclusions – in the Public Record Office soon comes to realise, there is a remarkable mixture in the content of such discussions: matters of urgency and importance may share a morning's agenda with relative trivia. Crossman (Howard 1979) records a Cabinet in 1965 at which the first item on the agenda was a museum to be built in the garden of the Royal Hospital at Chelsea. Vietnam, then the subject of sharp political controversy in Britain, was discussed later and as an afterthought. What is omitted can be even more surprising. The choice is mainly that of the Prime Minister, though any other member of the Cabinet intent on raising a particular subject can usually expect eventual success.

The proportion of the government's business discussed by the full Cabinet depends on the political balance within that government and thus varies considerably, but the basic principle is obvious enough. Twenty busy ministers make an unwieldy forum for the detailed discussion of any issue that is complex, contentious or urgent. As the business of government has expanded, it has become increasingly necessary both to reduce the proportion of proposals submitted to the Cabinet and to simplify the nature of the decisions required. If the Cabinet actually discuss a proposal, instead of delegating it or giving it the formal approval which convention or precedent seem to require from no less authoritative a source, this usually suggests that the issue is politically sensitive. Either the views of important ministers are divided and need to be reconciled or else trouble is expected – inside Parliament or elsewhere. Whatever the cause of friction, it can best be lubricated if discussion convinces ministers of the wisdom of Lord Melbourne, Queen Victoria's first Prime Minister, who once ended a

Cabinet meeting with the question: 'Now, is it to lower the price of corn, or isn't it? It is not much matter which we say, but mind, we must all say the same.'

If full Cabinet discussion of some particular issue does not appear to the Prime Minister as an essential condition for the support of his colleagues, he may prefer to remit it to a committee of the Cabinet or even to get a few ministers together for an informal talk. Practical men believe that reducing the number of those consulted usually reduces the number of objections as well, particularly if those consulted are carefully chosen.

There are always numerous Cabinet Committees. Some are to be found, with occasional changes of title, under any British government: for instance, on economic policy, on defence and overseas policy, on legislation. Others are set up by one government and dropped or radically altered by the next. Many come into existence only to cope with some transitory problem and are later disbanded. All Cabinet Committees have three characteristics in common. First, their composition, chairmanship and terms of reference are decided by the Prime Minister. Secondly, extraordinary efforts are made to keep these particulars secret, not only from the public, media and parliament, but from junior ministers, most officials and, in some cases, even other members of the Cabinet. The committee established in 1945 by Attlee to handle the British nuclear programme was disguised as GEN 75.

In that case, as in some others, there was a genuine anxiety to keep foreign governments in ignorance of what was being discussed. The main motive for secrecy, however, is domestic. No Prime Minister wishes it to be generally known – and this reluctance is usually fostered by officials of the Cabinet Office – which colleagues are regarded (and, still more, which are not) as best able to contribute to policy formation beyond the bounds of their departmental responsibility. Still less is it desired to invite and focus lobbying by revealing some of the subjects being discussed or which ministers are concerned. Of course, these rational preoccupations assume a feverish character under the influence of that cult of secrecy which is the chronic infection of the British governmental system. Although a newspaper may occasionally publish a conjectural list of Cabinet Committees, full and accurate knowledge is usually confined to a small minority of ministers and officials, most of the latter being in the Cabinet Office.

It is the backing of this organisation that is the third general characteristic of Cabinet Committees. Curiously enough, even the

Cabinet itself had no secretariat until 1916. When Lloyd George, the Prime Minister who had initiated the practice, fell from power in 1922, a serious effort was made to abolish the secretariat as being unconstitutional. Discussions among ministers, it was argued, ought to take place in the absence of officials, whose job was simply to carry out ministerial decisions after these had been reached in confidential consultation. The attempt failed because most politicians were well aware that, in the absence of any written record, earlier Cabinet meetings had sometimes left ministers uncertain what it was that they had actually agreed on.

The new system was put to an unexpected test in 1924. Ramsay MacDonald's Labour Government lost a vote of confidence on 8 October. The House of Commons had not accepted the Prime Minister's assurance that he had been in no way concerned in the withdrawal of a prosecution for sedition. On 3 December the new Conservative Government discovered from the minutes that the Cabinet had actually decided this issue on 6 August and that MacDonald had thus lied to the House. Though tempted, they refrained from exploiting their find for fear of creating 'a most unfortunate precedent'. The general interest of the governing class had transcended its ideological division.

Nowadays incoming ministers would not be exposed to such temptation: the permanent civil servants who staff the Cabinet secretariat would automatically withhold the secrets of earlier ministers. In July 1986 the Thatcher Government had to obtain the consent of James Callaghan before they could examine the papers on which his Labour Government had based their decision in 1977 to order the NIMROD early warning aircraft that were still not ready in 1986.

Nevertheless the constitutional argument is still not quite dead. The winter of 1985–6, when controversy was excited by the role played by the Secretary to the Cabinet in a minor political crisis that precipitated the resignation of two Cabinet Ministers, was not the only occasion when the activities of senior officials attracted the unwelcome glare of partisan publicity.

Crossman's diary as a Cabinet Minister (Howard 1979) contains constant complaints that, from 1964 to 1970, the Cabinet Office were able to organise a bureaucratic manipulation of the work of Cabinet and its committees as well as reinforcing the ability of the Prime Minister to dominate his colleagues. The Cabinet Office (much enlarged and strengthened since its origin as a mere secretariat) is not

How Cabinet and Commons Operate   49

formally a Prime Minister's Department, such as exists in some countries: Australia, for instance. In principle its function is to serve the Cabinet by coordinating preparations for their discussions, by recording and circulating their decisions and by ensuring that these are implemented. In practice the Cabinet Office (which has a communicating door into 10 Downing Street), looks to the Prime Minister to interpret the wishes of the Cabinet and to issue the instructions which officials will implement with due regard to the corporate policies and interests of the bureaucracy.

So, at least, many politicians assert. Crossman's own experience as a Cabinet Minister, though impairing his faith in the overwhelming power of the Prime Minister (he often complains of Wilson's inability to impose any strategy on his divided Cabinet) generated a new conspiracy theory (which has Conservative as well as Labour supporters) about the 'hidden hand' of the civil service. Nor can it be denied that many administrative practices ostensibly intended to improve the efficiency of Cabinet government also have the effect of reinforcing the authority of the Prime Minister and the influence of bureaucratic advice. Much business concerning the European Communities, intelligence assessments and (until the Central Policy Review Staff was abolished) organised foresight has been centralised in the Cabinet Office to the detriment of departmental ministers. These have also felt their individual authority threatened by the corporate advice emanating from the interdepartmental committees of officials established to match the various Cabinet Committees of ministers.

Yet it can be argued that the constant endeavour of officials to reach agreement among themselves on a collective policy for the government as a whole (not something that comes naturally to most politicians) is not only helpful to ministers, but necessary if public business is to be conducted in any orderly manner. Nor is it obvious that the many private and informal meetings which most Prime Ministers have with different groups of their colleagues are any more constitutional and democratic than the proceedings of a Cabinet Committee, even if the latter's conclusions are recorded by a civil servant.

What can scarcely be disputed is the need for the authority of the Cabinet to be delegated. Given the size of the population, Britain has a remarkably centralised government. There is no British equivalent to the States of the United States or of Australia, to the provinces of Canada or to the Länder of Federal Germany. Scotland has different laws and its own legal system; Northern Ireland is separately administered. Otherwise the Kingdom really is United. Local government has strictly limited powers and responsibilities and such autonomy as it ever had has been further reduced in recent years.

The most obvious form of delegation is to individual ministers in charge of particular government departments. How much one of them can decide on his own varies and is always hard to define. If legislation is involved or other departments affected, there must naturally be prior consultation. So there must be in other cases suggested by precedent, by convention or by the rules of procedure which Prime Ministers usually take an early opportunity of circulating to their Cabinet. Some Prime Ministers allow greater latitude than others – not least to some of their colleagues – and some ministers are able to demand it. Doubts can be resolved by discreet enquiries through officials, particularly private secretaries, but the individual minister is expected to exercise his judgement: a Whitehall euphemism for sensing what one can get away with. Some ministers manage more than others but none, if challenged, can claim independence of the Cabinet.

The authority concentrated in the Cabinet is even employed to influence those organisations supposed to exercise some control over the Executive: Parliament and Party. Cabinets normally include two members whose main duty is to act as Leader, respectively, of the House of Lords and the House of Commons. These Leaders are responsible, in consultation with the Opposition, for arranging the business of each House. The Leader of the House of Commons, in particular, is very much the dominant figure in deciding the parliamentary agenda – as the representative of the Cabinet.

Conservative governments have also tended to include among their Cabinet Ministers the Party Chairman, who is charged with the organisation of the faithful in the country at large rather than simply in Parliament. A Conservative Prime Minister still leads the party, but the Chairman does the organising and the propaganda. In the Labour Party the Chairman is not appointed by the Prime Minister and the Party's National Executive Committee is less submissive than the Conservative equivalent, but often also less satisfied. But all Cabinets are sometimes attended by the Chief Whip, who marshals the government's supporters in the House of Commons, even if he is not usually a Cabinet Minister. He has the rather humble title of Parliamentary Secretary to the Treasury, but is often reckoned a Minister of Cabinet rank.

These ministers are no mere liaison officers, for the House of

Commons is not an independent legislature of the kind envisaged by theorists of the separation of powers. Since 1713, for instance, only ministers have been allowed to introduce legislation that would entail raising taxes or increasing expenditure. This removes from the House of Commons some of the scope for initiative so notably enjoyed by the Congress of the United States, where the President sometimes has to veto the enactment of unsolicited expenditure. Naturally the House of Commons retains the right to *reduce* spending, but its exercise is a direct attack on the government of the day. Indeed, a motion to reduce a minister's salary by a token amount is one of the conventional gambits of the Opposition. Its success would entail the resignation of the minister and probably of the entire government.

It follows that the Government must take the lead in arranging the business of the House. They do not have an entirely free hand. On four days a week time is reserved for the questioning of ministers; on 20 Fridays for the introduction of bills by private members. The Opposition can choose the subject for debate on their 29 Supply Days or obtain additional time for a motion of censure. Any member who can persuade the Speaker that he has a matter of urgent public importance to raise may seek to move the adjournment of the House to discuss it. And a substantial slice of parliamentary attention is pre-empted by automatic debates on such recurring subjects as the Budget and Finance Bill. So the Leader of the House never thinks he has enough time for the business of government.

But the Cabinet have the advantage. Not only does government business normally enjoy priority in the House of Commons, but it is difficult for anyone else to seize the initiative. The Leader of the Opposition (a post paid from public funds), other opposition parties or private members must usually react to the legislation proposed, the statements made or the actions taken by the Government. Even this limited role of subjecting the conduct of the Government to critical scrutiny has become increasingly difficult for the House of Commons. The extent, variety and chronic urgency of governmental activities and responsibilities have throughout the twentieth century tended to outgrow the parliamentary resources available for controlling them. There is more legislation to be passed and less time for the House of Commons to discuss it in detail.

The House of Commons can influence the Executive in two main ways: by voting or by vexing.

Voting is the strongest weapon, but also the easiest for the Government to parry. All legislation and many executive acts (for instance, the annual Order in Council extending the duration of the Army Act) must be endorsed by a majority of those members present and voting. In the case of legislation a long succession of positive votes may be needed over a period of weeks in order to get just one bill through the Commons and up to the Lords. A single failure can be enough to arrest the passage of the bill and, on occasion, even to threaten the survival of the Government.

Nor are governments vulnerable to voting only when they take the initiative by introducing legislation. The procedure of the House of Commons gives the Opposition ample opportunity to force both a debate and a vote and such challenges sometimes present greater perils. A government incurring an adverse vote during the passage of legislation can often survive by accepting an amendment, dropping a clause or even abandoning a bill. After a vote of censure resignation may be the only option.

Governments usually avoid being voted down, let alone voted out, by using the Party Whips to mobilise the votes of their own supporters. No secret voting or proxy voting is permitted. Members are counted as they go through a door, as if they were sheep being dipped, into either the 'aye' or the 'no' lobby. Party discipline is strict. One story has been told so often in the last century and a half that it must sometimes have been true. The Chief Whip, watching a semi-conscious member being carried into the House on a stretcher, remarks to his Assistant: 'It doesn't matter if he dies – the seat is safe – but vote he must.'

Naturally the system is not infallible. The Whips are sometimes defied; governments occasionally have to change course; in 1940 Chamberlain resigned because many of his supporters would not vote for him; in 1979 the Callaghan Government were brought down by a single defection. In the future, coalition governments or minority governments will probably be as vulnerable as in the past. But a government with a decent majority must be incompetent or unlucky to be defeated on an important issue in the House of Commons. A member voting against his party's government in such circumstances is at least risking his future political career.

Vexing the Government does less damage than voting, but is harder to prevent. Exploiting parliamentary procedure to obstruct legislation or other essential business can admittedly be stopped, at some slight cost in popularity or prestige, by mobilising the government's majority to vote the closure of debate: the so-called 'guillotine', a device introduced at the end of the last century to cope with the tactics employed by Irish members. But there is only one impediment to the

How Cabinet and Commons Operate 53

ability of members of the House of Commons to embarrass the government by the questions put to ministers, by charges or disclosures in debate or through proceedings in committee. That impediment is ignorance. If ministers can keep their conduct secret, it will often escape effective challenge in the House. Anyone with experience in drafting replies to parliamentary questions knows that members are easily frustrated as long as they lack enough information to force the Minister into disclosing more. Over the last two decades successive governments have reluctantly acquiesced in the demand, from all parties, that the House of Commons should be better equipped to scrutinise the conduct of the Executive. In some countries, of course, the Legislature could have decided this on their own.

Members once provided with no more than a locker for their papers have gradually acquired offices (though not on the premises) and allowances for the employment of staff. The number of committees of the House of Commons has greatly increased (14 extra under Margaret Thatcher alone) and these committees have exposed the work of the Executive to more regular and systematic examination than was previously possible.

Nevertheless, when the facilities, accommodation, staff, salary and allowances of the British Member of Parliament are compared with those of the United States Congressman, the contrast is startling. In financial terms the ratio is about one to twenty. Nor is it only on the banks of the Potomac that the grass is greener. In 1985 (when restrictions were proposed) French legislators were still able to enjoy pluralism on the scale of the eighteenth-century Church, adding to their national emoluments such varied benefices as membership of the European Parliament, chairmanship of a regional council and a mayoralty, each with its particular perquisites. Within the building of the Finnish Parliament there is a luxurious bed-sitting room for every member. In the House of Commons, by one of the odder English traditions, there are not even enough seats in the Chamber for all the members.

The House of Commons, so critics contend, lacks the resources to do its job with full efficiency. But is it still, in Bagehot's sense of the word, an efficient rather than a dignified part of the political system?

One test is the ability of members to vex the Executive. Harold Macmillan, lately Lord Stockton, confessed to feeling physically sick before answering questions as Prime Minister, in the House of Commons. Permanent Under Secretaries, enjoying more pay, power and job security than many Members of Parliament will ever know, pass uneasy nights before giving evidence to a Select Committee. To be worsted in debate, to be heckled by one's own side, even to encounter only the sullen silence of government supporters can be painful experiences for ministers. This is an ordeal from which the President of the United States is as immune as Mr Gorbachev, but to which the British Prime Minister is always liable.

More than personal susceptibilities are involved, though it is arguably for the public good that these should be at risk. The survival of governments depends on the discipline of their supporters in the House. That discipline can be eroded if the Opposition are often able to make Ministers appear, even to ministerialists, as feeble, fools or knaves.

The practical importance of vexing ministers should not be exaggerated, but it would be no less mistaken to suppose that the House of Commons can influence governments only by voting them down or out. The privileged freedom of speech enjoyed by Members of Parliament enables them to expose scandal without need of legal proof or fear of legal process. The adversarial character of the House of Commons, in which Government and Opposition face each other across a gangway just too wide for drawn swords to meet, provides an added incentive. This helps to check some abuses of the power so tightly and so secretively concentrated in the British Executive.

Perhaps both the weaknesses and the strength of the House of Commons may be explained by its most distinctive characteristic: the intimacy of ministerial participation. It weakens because it impairs the independence and scope for initiative of the House, allowing the Executive to reinforce party discipline by the pay-roll vote and the temptations of office. It is partly because of ministerial participation that the House offends some members by meeting in the afternoons and sitting so late, thus leaving ministers free to attend their departments in the mornings. And even so, conscientious ministers are overburdened, not just by attendance at the House, but by the work required of an ordinary member wishing to be re-elected.

It is a strength not only that ministers must personally propose their measures and defend their conduct in the House, but also that the House can offer ministers some slight alleviation of their dependence on the Prime Minister. In the United States, members of the Cabinet are entirely the creatures of the President. If their British counterparts enjoy any status of their own, the main cause is their membership of the House of Commons.

How Cabinet and Commons Operate

Political power in Britain is, to an unusual degree, concentrated in the hands of a highly centralised government, who also exercise more control over the legislature than is customary in some countries. This Executive shows a marked preference for operating behind closed doors, but is nevertheless not immune from the questioning, the criticism, the opposition and, in some cases, the constraints exercised by the House of Commons. These constraints are less frequent and less obvious than they were a hundred years ago. Party discipline, the financial dependence of members and pressure of business have helped governments to bridle the House of Commons. But the harness is not fully dependable and the House, though far from being an ideal legislature, has not yet ceased to be an efficient rather than a dignified part of the constitution.

6 The Servants of the State

The decisions reached by the Cabinet and the laws passed by Parliament are carried out by a host of functionaries: civil servants and diplomats; sailors, soldiers and airmen; policemen and coastguards; judges and magistrates; inspectors of factories and inspectors of customs. Most modern states have this kind of administrative infrastructure and few could be governed without the services of men and women who, being under authority, interpret, apply and enforce the policies of the Executive and the laws of the Legislature.

The unusual feature of the British system – it is not unique, but it is unusual – is that nearly all these functionaries are permanently employed and without political affiliations. They are expected to serve the State and to obey those who control the State without regard to the political colour of either Executive or Legislature and irrespective of their individual political views, which, in many cases, they are precluded from expressing in public. In return for serving governments of all political complexions, they expect that all governments will continue to employ them.

When we talk of permanent employment, there are naturally differences between one kind of public servant and another. Judges, for instance, are chosen from the ranks of practising lawyers and are at least middle-aged before they are appointed, but do not have to retire before they are 70 or even 75. High Court judges, once appointed by the Lord Chancellor, can only be removed by the Sovereign after an address from both Houses of Parliament. More junior judges can be removed by the Lord Chancellor, but cases are rare. On the other hand, members of the armed forces start very early, but serve for fixed terms, except for officers, who are retired on a pension if they fail to achieve certain ranks by specified ages. For civil servants and diplomats the general rule is retirement at 60. Constitutionally, of course, all these functionaries except High Court judges are only employed during the Queen's pleasure and can be dismissed for misconduct or prematurely retired on grounds of diminished efficiency or because of some reduction in the size of the armed forces or the public service. But none of them lose their jobs simply because there has been a change of government.

There are similar differences in their political disqualification. Full-time judges, civil servants, diplomats and members of the armed

The Servants of the State

forces must resign before presenting themselves as candidates for election to Parliament. But the unpaid magistrates who hear 90 per cent of all criminal cases may be members of parliament. Indeed, when magistrates are appointed an effort is made to preserve a rough balance among the political parties. In 1977 34 per cent of them were supposed to be Conservative, 31 per cent Labour and 14 per cent Liberal, though the more conservative members of all parties are said to stand a better chance of being chosen. Otherwise the servants of the state are expected to avoid overt involvement in political activities, and the more senior they are, the more strictly the rule is applied.

Sixty years ago it was laid down, and the principle is still maintained, that the first duty of a civil servant is to give his undivided allegiance to the State. His abstention from partisan political activity is one side of the bargain. The other is that the State should not discriminate among its servants on political grounds. There has been some erosion of both principles since about 1950, but they are still broadly respected.

In 1985 Britain had half a million civil servants (the total has been falling for forty years). If the governing class is broadly defined, they should all be considered members, but even the narrowest definition must include the 2500-odd in what used to be called the Administrative Grade. These are the people who can expect, in the course of their active career, to make some contribution to policy formation. Most of them work in London, where they suggest to ministers what they should decide and how these decisions, whether originating as ministerial or as official ideas, might best be implemented.

This kind of bureaucratic influence is commonplace. What is exceptional is the British concept of a politically neutral bureaucracy. It is not only in politically volatile states that the practice is different. There an election, still more a *coup d'état*, may cost even the doorkeepers and the chauffeurs of government departments their jobs, because every salaried post is required for the supporters of the new regime and their dependants.

There may be more permanence in states dominated by a single party, sect or tribe, but there is no pretence at political neutrality. On the contrary, the condition of employment is undivided allegiance to an unchanging ruling class, perhaps even to a single ruler.

Even those industrialised democracies which seek to combine the stability of the state with the freedom of different political parties to compete for control of its government seldom fully endorse the British concept of a permanent and politically neutral infrastructure. Almost every country in Western Europe, for instance, recruits its armed forces by conscription, less for supposed military advantage than in the hope of making these forces politically representative. Professional armies are still regarded with some of the suspicion they aroused in seventeenth-century Britain.

In the United States every American Ambassador must automatically submit his resignation after a Presidential election and a new President can be expected to replace many of them as well as numerous senior officials in Washington. Nor are changes confined to the capital. Throughout the country sheriffs, judges, district attorneys and others are whirled away, dead leaves in the autumnal gale of innumerable elections.

Even in France, where the civil and diplomatic services are professionally established, a new government can bring changes even over and above the new Minister's personal team of ardent partisans to run his private office and dominate his Department. The legendary hierarchy of the Quai d'Orsay can be ordered about by bright young men, there or in the Elysée (office of the President). Much the same happens in Australia. In Finland the political affiliations of senior officials are well known and a conscious effort is made to maintain an appropriate political balance in most government departments. Communists, however, are not welcomed in the Ministries of Defence or Foreign Affairs.

I have not myself encountered another country in which such a clear distinction is maintained, as it is in Britain, between the elected politician, who becomes a minister and gives the orders, and the permanently appointed, unpolitical official who carries them out. Even in local government there are elected town councillors to decide municipal policy and officials appointed on a long term basis to carry it out.

There are many arguments, even within Britain itself, for and against this system and it would be foolish to insist that it is necessarily better or worse than that of other states. So much depends on differences in national traditions, culture, temperament. The British system itself is not much more than a century old. Before that public servants were appointed by patronage, a practice that led to growing complaints of nepotism and incompetence. Recruitment by competitive examination and promotion by professionally assessed merit were then regarded as, and proved to be, better than entry by political favouritism and automatic advance by seniority. Now the complaints are that the permanent servants of the State are too cautious, too addicted to compromise, incapable of responding with enthusiasm to demands for the sudden introduction of radical changes.

There is one form of change, however, to which civil servants do try to adapt: whenever the British government of the day announces that a general election is going to be held in a few weeks (three is the minimum interval). With the permission of the existing Prime Minister, the Secretary of the Cabinet, the most important permanent official in Britain, then gets in touch with the Leader of the Opposition and, if the political situation at the time warrants it, with the leaders of other major parties as well. The purpose is to ascertain informally what important changes of policy these parties would wish to introduce if they won the election and were able to form a government.

This conversation may be followed by others between the Permanent Secretaries of particular Departments and various politicians designated by the Leader of the Opposition as potential ministers. The manifestos and public declarations of the political parties are also studied and, on this basis and on that of the information given to them in confidence, the Permanent Secretaries of the various Departments then produce a range of policy options for the different governments that might emerge from the general election.

I was twice responsible for organising this task while I was Head of the Planning Staff in the Foreign Office. The resulting two-inch thick pile of paper was on the desk of every incoming minister on the morning of his arrival. It was a statement, both general and, in relation to particular countries and problems, detailed, of existing British foreign policy and, where appropriate, of the scope for the kind of change incoming ministers were believed to favour. On no other occasion did I ever see so comprehensive a written statement of British foreign policy.

Ministers read it carefully, sometimes more than once, in their first week or two. After that – the best of papers tend to be swept away in the gale of the world.

Tony Benn (1981) regards this practice with some suspicion as the presentation of 'the department's policy, which officials hope the new minister will follow . . . dressed up to look like a range of options for implementing the new government's manifesto.' It may still be better than the hurried meetings in a Washington hotel room, which the memoirs of American Presidential advisers have described, between bewildered academics and the ignorant organisers of elections.

Of course, at the very outset, there is one element in the ethos of the permanent British bureaucracy that soon begins to irritate new ministers. The bureaucracy see themselves as the guardians of the national interest. There is policy – and they are scrupulous in indicating its possible variants – the median line about which successive governments are free to zig-zag. But it is also a median line, so they discreetly but persistently insinuate, from which any government would be rash to make a radical departure.

Historically, of course, British governments leaving the middle of the road have sometimes ended in the ditch. But the bureaucratic attitude derives from the belief that they know more about the practical tasks of government than any politician mainly occupied in making speeches and kissing the babies of the electorate. Secondly, they think that their job security and political neutrality enable them to put the country first, to see the long-term perspective, to represent the enduring national interest. These opinions are unwelcome to many politicians, but are particularly objectionable to the radicals of both Left and Right.

The conflict between politicians and officials should nevertheless not be exaggerated. Ministers may feel themselves the latest and best choice of the electorate; be conscious of the extent of needed change and the shortage of time for its achievement. Officials may cherish their secret and sacred responsibility for maintaining the fabric and continuity of the State. In practice they usually get on well enough, the former accepting advice and the latter orders.

There are, however, certain conventions that occasionally cause friction. The recruitment, transfer and promotion of officials are processes over which, except at the highest levels, ministers exercise little control. Some of them would like more power to 'hire and fire'. The relationship between officials and the special advisers whom ministers nowadays tend to recruit from their own political party can be uneasy. And the distinction officials try to draw between their unstinted service to ministers in running the country and their abstention from vote-catching activities is often both artificial and, as ministerial memoirs suggest, irritating.

Another unusual convention is that the records of ministerial decisions are kept by officials, who remain their sole custodians on a change of government. The American practice, whereby an outgoing President carries away with him all his official papers and uses them to create a library bearing his own name, is actually a crime in Britain under the Official Secrets Acts. An ex-minister who wants to write his memoirs is allowed access to his own papers in the official archives, but must submit the resulting typescript to the Secretary of the Cabinet for scrutiny and approval before publication. An attempt to apply this

The Servants of the State

censorship to the private diary kept by Crossman (Howard 1979) of his activities as a Cabinet Minister led to a monumental row and some enlargement of the bounds of permissible publication, but the requirement is still in force today.

What all this adds up to is that the British State has a major new component since Bagehot wrote his book in 1867 (Crossman 1963): not just Queen, Cabinet and Parliament, but also the Civil Service. Of course, civil servants obey the orders of ministers, just as the Queen accepts their advice. But the existence of an independent, professional, permanent hierarchy, with its own collective views, its internal discipline and its particular sense of corporate loyalty, means that there is in Britain a fourth source of political influence and even power. Its importance has been steadily augmented by two modern developments: the ever-growing volume and complexity of public business and the proliferating requirements of security.

Until nearly the end of the nineteenth century, for instance, British Foreign Secretaries personally conducted British foreign policy, themselves writing all important instructions to British diplomatic representatives abroad. The staff of the Foreign Office were little more than clerks: filing papers, copying papers, cyphering and decyphering, attending to formalities, looking up treaties and precedents when required. Even the Permanent Under-Secretary (who has a different title from a Permanent Secretary only because the latter does not have a Secretary of State as his chief) played no part in policy formation, offering advice only if asked. All that has utterly changed, in the Foreign Office and in other government departments, where the pressure of work has become so great that policy must, for the most part, be proposed as well as executed by officials.

As for security, something of an obsession in Britain, there have never been so many secrets nor such an effort to restrict the numbers of those with access to them. As a result many secrets are known to some officials, yet concealed from most ministers. The so-called 'need to know' principle may have originated as a security precaution, but it has become an instrument of political power.

That officials should enjoy a degree of power is a source of grievance to many politicians. To some extent they have only themselves to blame. Margaret Thatcher was not the first Prime Minister to demonstrate that officials can be cowed as well as controlled, nor has the lion-tamer's role been assumed by Prime Ministers alone. Any minister sure of what he wants and able to take decisions can manage it. If bureaucratic power exists, it is partly because such ministers are exceptional and because the mutual loyalty of politicians does not match that of civil servants.

The armed forces, as already mentioned, are unusual because they are voluntarily enlisted professionals. Conscription has always been regarded with repugnance in Britain and has been sparingly employed even in wartime. Last introduced in 1939, it had nevertheless to be maintained for a number of years after the end of the Second World War because of the numerous conflicts entailed by the dissolution of the British Empire. It was abolished in 1960. Constitutionally, Navy, Army and Air Force are all the Forces of the Crown, but there is no Commander-in-Chief and political control is exercised by the Cabinet through the Ministry of Defence. The armed forces have played no part in British politics since 1914, when a number of army officers resigned their commissions under the mistaken impression that the British government of the day intended to use the Army in order to coerce the people of Ulster into joining an independent Ireland ruled from Dublin. This incident, rather dramatically known as the Curragh Mutiny, was largely the fault of the Government, who had ignored warnings from King George V of the risks they were running. The incident was quickly smoothed over and there has been no similar occurrence in the nineteenth and twentieth centuries.

The organisation of the British police is complex, confusing and often contradictory. In principle there is no national police force (a concept traditionally regarded as oppressive), but 52 regional forces. In London the Metropolitan Police (as distinct from the small, separate force in the financial district called the City of London) are directly controlled by the Home Secretary and in Ulster the police come under the Secretary of State for Northern Ireland. The Special (political) Branch is part of the Metropolitan Police, though most of its members now serve with provincial forces. In 1987, when the BBC in Glasgow were raided by the Special Branch, it was to the Commissioner of the Metropolitan Police that the Chairman of the BBC complained. The Security and Secret Intelligence Services are directly responsible to Ministers. But the remaining 49 police forces in England, Scotland and Wales are each commanded by a Chief Constable, who is personally responsible for their operations, and administered by a regional Police Authority composed of elected Councillors from the relevant local government areas and magistrates.

In practice the powers enjoyed by the Home Secretary and the Secretary of State for Scotland to approve the choice of senior officers, to set uniform conditions of service and training, to inspect the regional forces and to make various regulations produce a high degree of standardisation. The influence of central government is further increased by paying half the cost of all these forces. In 1984 and 1985 the widespread violence engendered by the strike of the National Union of Mineworkers was met by deploying police reinforcements from all over the country to the trouble spots. In emergencies, therefore, these separate police forces are so easily coordinated that they amount in practice to something very like a national force.

In more normal times, however, the autonomy of the separate Chief Constables is real and, in principle, police operations outside London are not subject to political direction from the capital. Chief Constables are expected to enforce the law impartially and on their own responsibility, but may be, and sometimes are, criticised by their Police Authority.

The character and functions of the British police have, however, considerably altered during the last fifty years as a result of the ever increasing incidence of crime and, more particularly, of politically motivated crime, terrorism and civil disturbances. The increase in ordinary crime has led to greater coordination and to the routine adoption of more forceful responses by the police. The latter is an even more obvious reaction to the rise in political violence and has caused some sections of British society to look on the police as not merely the agents of the Law, but as the defenders of the State and upholders of the status quo. The police have thereby been drawn into political controversy to a greater extent than in former times.

Of course, even in earlier years, when crime was mostly directed against property, the police were inevitably more popular with those who had property than with those who had not. But active suspicion and resentment of the police were then confined to rather a small minority. Most British people then regarded their policemen as more deserving of respect than those of other countries. In 1947 such a radical writer as George Orwell could assert that 'the police have public opinion behind them'. Even in the fifties and sixties we used to congratulate ourselves that our police were unarmed, that we had no riot squads, that our policemen were friendly, themselves respected the law and always employed minimum force. Today, in the deteriorating conditions of modern times, we must reluctantly admit that our police are coming to resemble those of other industrialised democracies.

The organisation of the judiciary has already been mentioned, but there are two further ways in which British practice differs from that of other countries. In Britain all judges and magistrates are appointed and not, unlike many in the United States, elected. Nor is there in Britain, as there is in many European countries, a judicial profession. Judges are selected from the ranks of lawyers in private practice and most magistrates, the so-called justices of the peace, are laymen (or women).

The law in Scotland, incidentally, is not the same as in the rest of the United Kingdom, but shares one characteristic which distinguishes the British system from that of many countries: the adversary principle. Every case, criminal or civil, is a contest between two sides. The function of the Court is not to discover the truth, but to hold the ring, to see that the rules are observed and to let the best man win. Law in Britain also resembles the constitution in having multiple sources, in its lack of certainty and in its reliance on precedent. There is no equivalent of the Code Napoléon.

The law in Britain is by and large the servant of the State – less than in the Soviet Union, more than in the United States – rather than its rival. Of course, the innocent are mostly acquitted and, according to the police, so are many of the guilty. A foreigner stands a better chance in Britain than in most countries I know of winning a case against a native inhabitant. Judges do occasionally pounce on abuses of power by the Executive and, as already mentioned, juries will refuse to convict if they consider the law to be unjust or oppressively applied. In 1985 a surprising number of the miners charged with riot during a strike that was violent – as we all saw on television – as well as unpopular, were acquitted.

The provision of legal aid has given many (but not all) poor litigants as privileged a position as the really rich: at the expense of those in between. But the general bias of the law in Britain is to uphold the State and the Executive and the rights of Property. Perhaps it is not fundamentally so different elsewhere.

It is, of course, often argued by left-wing politicians that all the established servants of the State are inevitably biased against socialist policies by their class origins and that their supposed political neutrality is a fiction. This is a contention to be approached with caution. It is true enough that anyone who has achieved membership of the governing class in any country cannot be expected to cooperate in the kind of change that would revolutionise the character of the state or the composition of the governing class. The old myth about the Monarch being constitutionally obliged to sign his or her own death warrant has not even been suggested as applicable to the servants of the State. In Britain many of them, particularly in the armed forces and the Diplomatic Service, hold the Queen's Commission and have an additional motive for refusing compliance with revolutionary measures.

Some have argued that, even in less extreme contingencies, the social origins of the servants of the state are liable to impair their cooperation with the policies of a democratically elected Labour government. This is not a view shared by the many Conservative politicians inclined to regard civil servants as closet socialists. Nor are the data on social origins always reliable. A recent view (Moran 1985) that the Diplomatic Service was 'closed socially' and virtually unchanged since before the Second World War appeared to be based on a calculation that 76.3 per cent of ambassadors in 1983 had been educated at fee-paying schools. Even if this had been a reliable indicator of social origins, it could only have related to the fifties, when most people who were ambassadors in 1983 would have joined the service.

In any case, environment is arguably more important than heredity in determining the outlook of the governing class. Education is important in its own right rather than as an indicator of social origin. Nor does education end with school or university. As the officers of the civil and military services have become socially more mixed, increased emphasis has been laid on role-perpetuation: inculcating into new recruits the values of their predecessors. The important purpose of this indoctrination is preparation for the discharge of a particular function within the political structure of the governing class. But the minutiae are not neglected. At the Britannia Royal Naval College at Darmouth midshipmen practise passing the port round the table after dinner. In American military academies some of the initiatory rituals are even odder.

In Britain, therefore, the various servants of the State have two main characteristics. They are so organised as to reinforce the centralised and concentrated authority of the Executive. Not being themselves elected, they cannot pose any democratic challenge to the legitimacy of the Executive. Nevertheless, the corporate nature and partial autonomy of such disciplined organisations as the civil service, the armed forces and the police give them a degree of potential influence which the Executive cannot afford altogether to disregard. The government of the day have reliable servants, but servants who are neither slaves nor entirely dispensable. They count in the balance of political power.

7 The Rivals of the State

By rivals of the State I do not mean the enemies of the State: those who seek its destruction or its violent transformation or who are ready to betray it to a foreign power. The rivals are those organisations which do not give undivided allegiance to the State and still less to the persons who, at any given time, happen to control the State. In the exercise of what they see as their independent functions, these organisations offer to their adherents alternative sources of legitimacy and additional magnets for loyalty.

The most obvious rivals of the State are the political parties, but these will receive the separate treatment they deserve in Chapter 9. The rivals for discussion here are the trade unions, local government, multinational corporations, the media and the churches.

At the end of 1984 about 11 million British workers – 44 per cent of the work force – belonged to 371 trade unions; most of them to the 7 largest unions whose individual membership ranged from 0.25 million to 1.5 million. For instance, the Transport and General Workers Union had 1.5 million members; the Amalgamated Union of Engineering Workers 1.2 million and the General, Municipal, Boilermakers and Allied Trades Union 875 000. This proportion of union membership (lower now than it used to be) is rather higher than the international average, less than the 80 per cent in Sweden, but well above the 28 per cent in France or the 20 per cent in the United States. British unions tend to differ from many of their foreign counterparts because the most important of them are often amalgamations of smaller unions. Members of a single union may do quite different kinds of work and most industrial enterprises employ workers belonging to more than one union. The National Union of Mineworkers is often regarded as, exceptionally, a single union covering an entire industry, but even in the coalfields there are small separate unions for managerial and supervisory staff as well as the Union of Democratic Mineworkers, which broke away from the main union in 1985 after the big miners' strike of 1984–5.

It is a common experience, therefore, for one employer to have to negotiate with several different unions and for these unions to argue among themselves about which jobs belong by right to the members of which union. This is a frequent source of difficulty when new technology creates new kinds of job.

The Rivals of the State

Most unions belong to the Trades Union Congress (TUC), but this is more of a parliament than a government and can seldom exert much control over individual unions. Perhaps its most effective role is in preventing unions from competing against one another to recruit members. There is also a Scottish Trades Union Congress and a Northern Ireland Committee of the Irish Congress of Trades Unions, but many workers in these two countries belong to unions based in England or affiliated to the main Trades Union Congress. The eight TUC regional councils for England and the Wales Trades Union Council are of lesser status.

In many other countries rival unions and even rival federations of unions compete with one another, often in alliance with different political parties. In Britain there is only one important trade union movement and nearly all the bigger unions support the Labour Party, which the unions helped to create, which they largely finance and over which they exercise considerable influence. This does not prevent the existence of sharp political differences between one union and another and thus within the Trades Union Congress. The leadership of some unions is in Communist hands, others follow distinctly right wing policies and the rest reflect most shades of opinion between these two extremes. Among the rank and file, political enthusiasm is less conspicuous. Many trade unionists do not pay the political levy for the Labour Party (though most unions contribute to Labour Party funds) and in 1979 a third of them voted for the Conservatives.

British trade unions tend to be more concerned to preserve the jobs and improve the wages and working conditions of their members than with securing political change. Although they favour and support the Labour Party, a Labour Government that attempts to restrict wage increases or to discourage strikes may encounter almost as much union resistance as a Conservative Government. And no government has ever succeeded in imposing the kind of controlled national wage bargaining to be found, for instance, in the Nordic countries, where, as it happens, the system came under some strain in the strike season of 1986.

The trade unions, therefore, are an autonomous force operating on the left flank of British politics. They are certainly not the creatures of the Labour Party. On the contrary, if the unions were themselves less divided, the Labour Party would be their creature: in 1983, five-sixths of the centrally controlled income of the Labour Party came from the trade unions.

This autonomy is strengthened by the relative freedom (even after the laws passed under the Thatcher Government) from the kind of legal restrictions to be found in Germany, the United States or Canada. The legislative curbs envisaged in 1969 by the Wilson Government foundered on political opposition; those actually introduced by the Heath Government between 1970 and 1974 were forcibly frustrated by the trade unions. Indeed, when the Heath Government lost the 1974 election, to which they had resorted as a kind of appeal to the country against a successful strike by the National Union of Mineworkers, that union was established in a position of dominance which subsequent governments shrank from challenging until Margaret Thatcher, who had herself earlier preferred to appease the union, opted for confrontation in March 1984.

This led to civil violence more widespread and intensive than had been known in Great Britain for many years. From the outset the leaders of the National Union of Mineworkers made it clear that they considered themselves responsible to their members alone, although they refused to organise a ballot of the national membership, as the union's own rules seemed to require, before a strike was called. Arguments that some of their actions were illegal, even when endorsed by Court orders, were brushed aside with the comment that the leadership recognised only the decisions and regulations of the National Union of Mineworkers. The actions in which these leaders were supported by an apparent majority of miners demonstrated that the union was a rival to the State, an organisation offering an alternative source of legitimacy and commanding more loyalty from its members than they were willing, at least on this issue, to accord to the State.

The miners, to whose struggle we must return, because it is one of the more important developments in recent British politics, carried their defiance of the State to greater and more widespread extremes of violence than anyone else. But other unions have, from time to time, manifested their rivalry with the State by defying the Government (even Labour Governments) and the orders of the Courts. Some unions have emulated the miners, though never on the same scale, by organising mass pickets of many hundreds outside some factory or enterprise in order to intimidate workers from going to their jobs or other firms from having any dealings with the commercial concern in dispute with the union. And inconveniencing members of the public is a routine gambit: interrupting the supply of electricity or water; stopping the burial of the dead or interfering with the care of the sick.

The point at issue is not the merits of such disputes or of the tactics

The Rivals of the State

employed, but the special position of the trade unions in the British political system. This was well defined by Len Murray, formerly General Secretary of the Trades Union Congress:

> Trade unions claim that there are areas of activity in which they have an inherent right to act independently as opposed to that right being created by the state and thus subject to reappraisal and modification by the state.
>
> (Pimlott 1982)

The unions are true rivals of the State, because they consider the State has no right to interfere with the process of collective bargaining – which means mutual coercion – between employers and employed.

This process operates even among the servants of the State. Trade unions are illegal in the police and the armed forces and the Thatcher Government recently extended this principle to the electronic intelligence organisation known, with characteristically British ambiguity, as the Government Communications Headquarters. But there are some militant trade unions in the Civil Service. In 1986 striking prison officers frightened even themselves by the riots they provoked in the overcrowded gaols. The old, the sick, the poor and the unemployed are, from time to time, inconvenienced in the course of attempts by other unions to increase the salaries of their members.

There are still a few people in Britain who do not, unlike their counterparts elsewhere, go on strike: nurses, for instance. Many unions manage to promote the interests of their members without striking. It is not even true that Britain is the world's most strike-ridden country. Even in the bad years of the seventies and early eighties, the ratio of working days lost through strikes was often worse in Canada, the United States, Italy, Greece, Spain, Ireland and Australia. It was when we compared our figure of 500 days lost for every 1000 workers with Switzerland's 5 days that we had to hang our heads in shame. Under the Thatcher Government, once the miners' strike was over, there has even been some improvement, the year ending May 1986 being the best since 1967.

Moreover, if the leaders of British trade unions often have political motives, they are free from the links with organised crime established in the United States. Nor are they, as is the case in the Soviet Union, the puppets of the State. On the contrary, whenever British governments attempt to manipulate the British economy by exerting pressure on jobs or wages, the resistance of trade unions demonstrates the extent of their rivalry with the State and has, in the past, often caused their leaders to be compared to the barons of mediaeval England.

This rivalry was most dramatically apparent in the miners' strike of 1984–5, when the partly Communist union leadership were thought to be actuated by political motives, wanting to bring down the Thatcher Government as, ten years earlier, their predecessors had brought down the Heath Government. The ostensible cause was the Coal Board's strategy (encouraged by the government) of closing pits operating at a loss, though with generous compensation for those miners who could not find, or did not wish to be found, work at another pit. The implications of this strategy for the future of the industry and the impact on the close-knit mining communities would have been enough to arouse indignation even if the Coal Board had handled the issue, and an earlier pay claim, less clumsily. But the merits of the dispute were quickly overshadowed by the tactics employed in its prosecution.

Because the union leadership were not sure that a majority of their members would support a strike, they did not risk a national ballot. Instead they endorsed calls for a strike from Yorkshire and Scotland, hoping that other areas would follow suit and the strike spread by seemingly spontaneous combustion. Some areas did fall into line, but others held local ballots and voted against strike action. Many hundreds of miners were then despatched from the militant areas to form mass pickets at pits still working and to intimidate the recalcitrant into joining the strike. Violence sometimes ensued, as it did when similar tactics were employed against lorry drivers moving coal stocks.

The Government responded with an equally massive mobilisation and deployment of the police to protect those willing to produce and move coal. The Courts sequestrated the funds of the National Union of Mineworkers; other unions gave them, at best, half-hearted support; electricity generation (the key to success in previous coal strikes) was never interrupted; and the strike collapsed, a year after it had begun, without achieving any of the objectives of the union leadership. The cost to the country has been estimated at five billion pounds – much more than any likely subsidy for the continued operation of uneconomic pits.

As a conflict the strike resembled a war. Even those who won it would have done better if they had avoided it. But once it had begun and had been perceived as a violent challenge to the authority of the State, it was a conflict that had to be won if the Government was to

The Rivals of the State

survive and the supremacy of the State to be upheld. This was rivalry at its most extreme.

There are many potential rivals in local government, but none of such power: parish councils, district councils, county councils, city councils, metropolitan county councils. In Scotland there are even island councils. The largest and most important of all used to be the Greater London Council, now one of those dissolved in the latest instalment of the confusing and often contradictory organisational changes of the seventies and eighties.

All these councils are controlled by representatives – generally called councillors – elected in local elections quite separate, though on the same franchise, from those for the election of members of parliament. Their powers and duties (parish councils have few of either) include the provision of cheap housing for rent; care of the local environment; refuse collection and public health; amenities and recreational facilities; road maintenance and traffic control; the organisation of schools, police, fire and social services; the maintenance of public libraries. All within their own area.

The need for a distinction between national and local government is obvious enough and is acknowledged in most countries. Unfortunately British inability to impose logical patterns on the haphazard evolution of their social and political history has considerably blurred the practical application of this distinction. Local authorities were once autonomous: their revenue came from a tax (known as rates) which they were entitled to levy on the occupiers of buildings or other kinds of real estate. These ratepayers were then also the electors and the councillors they chose decided how the money they paid should be spent. Simple and democratic.

But the franchise was later extended and the poorer electors were exempted from the payment of rates. A conflict of interests ensued between those who paid and those who merely voted, but nevertheless expected. These rising expectations were increasingly subsidised from the funds of the central government, who themselves had a strong interest in ensuring that the hundreds of local authorities provided roughly uniform services. This interest was heightened when governments, particularly the Thatcher Government, became concerned to reduce their own expenditure. In 1977, for instance, grants to local authorities had accounted for nearly a quarter of central government expenditure and provided over half the revenue of the local authorities themselves. By the end of 1985 central funds were providing only 46 per cent of local expenditure.

The reluctance of local councillors to reduce the expenditure they regarded themselves as having been elected to carry out was aggravated when, as often happened, they belonged to a different political party. Local elections are increasingly fought under the banners of the national political parties. The years of the Thatcher Government have thus seen repeated efforts by councils with a Labour majority to spend more money than Conservative ministers were willing to permit. This municipal defiance has often extended to actions of doubtful legality and has entailed considerable inconvenience to members of the public. So far it has had little success, because councillors cannot count on the kind of mass loyalty generated by many trade unions. They can only hope that publicising their grievances will eventually alter the attitude or composition of the government and the House of Commons. In 1985, however, when the city of Liverpool had been brought to the brink of collapse by the intransigence of councillors trying to coerce the government into providing more money, no sympathy was forthcoming from the Labour Party or the trade unions. The ruling faction on the council belonged to the Militant Tendency (see Chapter 9). Their sense of rivalry with the State was as acute as Scargill's, but they lacked his muscle.

Multinational corporations are a problem in Britain, as they are elsewhere, because they do not owe undivided allegiance to the State, perhaps to any state. As some of them are sufficiently British to be important contributors to the national economy, it is hard for the British government to impose strict controls on the domestic activities of all multinationals. That is a course sometimes attempted, not always with much success, by governments for whom such corporations are wholly alien.

It is not only the ability of these corporations to escape their proper share of national taxation by transfer-pricing and similar devices that is disturbing. On occasion they have also been able to defy government policies of other kinds. During the period when Britain was applying the sanctions approved by the United Nations against the Smith regime in Rhodesia, supposedly British oil companies assisted the South African government to provide Rhodesia with clandestine supplies of oil. And more than one British government has found multinationals to be slippery customers when it comes to deciding what they shall invest or produce in Britain.

Admittedly, the Thatcher Government, whose respect for the freedom of commercial enterprise is exceptional in Britain, reacted sharply and decisively when the United States government tried to use American multinationals to prevent British firms from participating in the construction of the gas pipe-line between the Soviet Union and West Germany. It would nevertheless be optimistic to regard multinationals operating in Britain as adequately amenable to the authority of the British government. Probably only the European Economic Community has the power, if agreement could ever be reached on an effective policy, to bring these organisations under political control. Until that happens, if it ever does, multinational corporations are likely to remain – discreetly, of course – the rivals of the British state.

Corporations or other concentrations of capital wholly employed or owned in Britain do not come into the category of rivals to the State. Naturally their political influence (to be examined in later chapters) is quite as important as that of the trade unions, but it has to be exerted on and through the State. Unlike trade unions or the media, British corporations can neither claim mass support nor appeal directly to any significant proportion of the people. They have to operate within the ordinary political process and they have a special need for the protection of the State. Not only do they often depend, as multinationals do not, for their very survival on the goodwill of the British State: they are also much more exposed to its pressure.

In Britain the media, meaning the purveyors of news and political comment, share with the Executive the distinctive features of concentration and centralisation. The important newspapers are few in number, located in London and enjoy a nation-wide circulation. Scotland is a partial exception. The handful of owners, some of them families or even individuals, may also be identified among those who control provincial newspapers or commercial radio and television stations. The latter, no less than those of the publicly owned British Broadcasting Corporation, may in many respects have a regional, even a local character, but tend to take their main news and views from London.

By convention and sometimes by covenant proprietors do not exercise complete control. Editors have considerable independence and journalists much influence. Nevertheless the narrow ownership of the British media helps to explain why, if they are rivals to the State, they are so to a lesser degree than their counterparts in the United States. The British media have a privileged rather than a populist image. Nor do they enjoy the special position conferred on the American press by the Constitution of the United States.

On the contrary the media suffer from the relative severity of the law in Britain concerning official secrets, contempt of court and defamation. It can sometimes be more difficult in Britain than in some other countries to publish what cannot be proved or what the State or the powerful are concerned to hide.

Comment, however, is relatively free. Even the British Broadcasting Corporation, whose revenue is determined, as its governors are appointed, by the State, cannot be controlled in the way in which French television has been controlled by French governments. A rare attempt, in 1985, to prevent the showing of a programme considered indulgent towards terrorism in Ulster exposed the Thatcher Government to sharp public criticism. Indeed, governments of both parties have frequently complained of being unfairly treated on British television. Perhaps the Conservative Party tend to be rather more resentful of the attitudes displayed on television screens, just as the Labour Party regard most newspapers as biased against them.

Perhaps the dominant influence on the media comes from the journalists themselves. Most of them seem to have much the same sceptical, cynical, questioning and censorious attitude towards the State and the servants of the State as is to be found elsewhere. When combined with the compulsive need to turn everything into a sensational story, this professional irreverence is enough to make the media natural rivals of the State. It also helps to explain why, in November 1985, the House of Commons again refused to allow their proceedings to be televised.

On the international scale of democratic countries the strength of the British media as rivals to the State ranks well below that of their American counterparts, but is probably above average. There are very democratic countries where muck-raking is considered disreputable and the media are both more respectful and more respectable than in Britain. One contrast often drawn is that between the Falklands War, where the representatives on the spot of the British media were under relatively tight control (though never tight enough to satisfy the troops) and the Vietnam War, where American reporters often seemed to be accorded every facility and subjected to no restrictions. In both cases, of course, editors at home were free to criticise as they wished.

Over time, however, the readiness of the British media to challenge the State has significantly increased. In 1936, when the newspapers of other countries were full of stories and pictures of the liaison between

King Edward VIII and Mrs Simpson, the British media preserved complete silence until the political crisis was about to break. That would not happen today.

The nature of the British media may soon be modified by technology. The processes involved are not particularly new, but their political implications are novel. The conflict between innovating owners and conservative unions is not yet over, but it is already possible to see some chance of significantly lower costs and correspondingly wider newspaper ownership. The use of satellites and cable transmission may open British television to international competition and, incidentally, wider domestic access.

The choice of the churches as the final example of the rivals of the State reflects the perceptions of politicians rather than the realities of power. In recent years the prominence accorded to the public comments of church leaders on such subjects as nuclear weapons, Ulster, aid to the Third World, the miners' strike and the economic and social policies of the present government has aggrieved politicians ignorant of British history.

There has never been, in this country, the kind of separation between religion and politics prescribed in the Constitution of the United States or often attempted in France. The Church of England is 'by law established'; its bishops are appointed by the Monarch on the advice of the Prime Minister and have always been politically prominent. One of the earlier Archbishops of Canterbury, Ceolnoth, was mainly responsible, in AD 864, for the disastrous expedient of Danegeld – the payment of blackmail to Scandinavian raiders – which is usually blamed on King Ethelred the Unready. Political involvement brought many of his successors to a violent death.

Other sects have produced quite as many turbulent priests, but only in Ulster are they a peril to the State today. Twenty per cent would be a fairly high estimate of the proportion of the British population committed to any religion at all. But Churchmen do not give undivided allegiance to the State; their utterances irk politicians; they have some influence; they count as rivals – just.

The significance of these five rivals – trade unions, local government, multinational corporations, media and churches – to the State depends on their ability, which varies considerably, to restrain the freedom of action of a government supported by a majority in the House of Commons. At certain periods, and on some issues, one or other of them may become a factor in the balance of political power, almost a component of the virtual constitution.

Either trade unions or multinational corporations, for instance, could create a more substantial obstacle to the decisions of the Executive than anything to be expected from the Royal Veto or the House of Lords. Some grievances are more effectively ventilated by the media, the churches or even local government than in the House of Commons. Purists may reject these rivals as elements of the constitution, but they belong to the political system.

Bagehot would not have been surprised. He argued that the British constitution, as he knew it, depended on the deference of the masses towards their rulers. The influence of these rivals of the State is one expression of the decline of that deference.

8 The Commonwealth

Very few people in Britain and even fewer elsewhere entirely understood the nature of the British Empire. Its successor, the Commonwealth, is still more complex and bewildering. It is, of course, one of the dignified parts of the constitution, as the Royal Style and Title make clear:

> Elizabeth the Second, by the Grace of God of the United Kingdom of Great Britain and Northern Ireland and of Her other Realms and Territories Queen, Head of the Commonwealth, Defender of the Faith etc. etc.

It is nevertheless an institution which has had, and which continues to have, important practical consequences for the British political system.

Naturally the Commonwealth, no less than other aspects of the British Constitution, is constantly evolving. A single chapter is altogether inadequate to describe a subject to which many writers have devoted volumes based on years of research, only to discover that what they have written is out of date before it is printed.

The subject must be simplified even at the cost of distortion by depicting the Commonwealth only as seen from the British Isles. The views of the remaining billion inhabitants will barely get a glance. This book can only accommodate the Commonwealth by concentrating on its impact on the British political system rather than on its position and influence in the world.

The name 'Commonwealth' – a curious choice in view of its association with the Cromwellian interregnum – seems to have had its origin in the formula adopted by the Imperial Conference of 1926 to define the relationship between Britain and what were then the six self-governing dominions of the British Empire:

> They are autonomous communities within the British Empire, equal in status, in no way subordinate to one another in any aspect of their domestic or internal affairs, though united by a common allegiance to the Crown, and freely associated as members of the British Commonwealth of Nations.

Everything that has happened since can be regarded as an extension or a modification of those principles, but the end result is rather different from anything envisaged in 1926. The six autonomous communities then mentioned – Australia, Canada, Ireland, Newfoundland, New Zealand and South Africa – were then only the tip of the enormous imperial iceberg, which extended to every continent and included innumerable dependencies whose different descriptions – empire, colony, protectorate, mandated territory – and various systems of administration did not conceal the fact that they were neither autonomous nor equal nor freely associated but, in the last resort, were ruled from London.

In sixty years all that enormous iceberg has dissolved and there is now no member of the Commonwealth – the adjective 'British' has gone – that is not freely associated and no territory that is ruled from London against the wishes of the majority of its inhabitants.

When the Commonwealth Heads of Government met in the Bahamas in October 1985, there were, including Britain, 49 independent members of the Commonwealth and around a dozen dependencies. The precise number depends on how the counting is done. For instance are St Helena, Ascension Island and Tristan da Cunha three dependencies or one? Of the former, 18 were monarchies acknowledging Queen Elizabeth II as their sovereign; 26 were republics of very various kinds; and 5 were monarchies with different sovereigns of their own. All accepted the Queen, who arrived for the occasion in the Royal Yacht *Britannia*, as Head of the Commonwealth.

These statistics will probably require amendment before this book emerges from the press. When that happens it will still be possible to spend an entire day interrogating pedestrians in Piccadilly without finding one who could reel off all 49 names.

Of all the complex and often contradictory impulses that went to make up this change, the process of decolonisation, which began after the Second World War, is perhaps the easiest to understand. The growth of nationalism in the dependent territories coincided with one international and two British developments. The international development was the disappearance, largely owing to Japanese successes before and during the Second World War, of the essential basis of the entire colonial system: the white man's prestige.

Prestige is no longer a fashionable concept, but it is important to remember that the British Empire was not held by force. Between the two world wars, for instance, 1300 British officials ruled 350 million

The Commonwealth

Indians with the assistance of one British soldier for every 6000 inhabitants. How many independent governments today, in any continent, could survive on that ratio of rulers to ruled? It was only possible in the old British Empire because of prestige and the deference that prestige inspired. When those went, the Empire had to follow.

The specifically British developments were the decline in relative economic and military strength (even prestige needed some backing) and the accelerating decay of the British imperial instinct. Revisionist historians have argued that, for most of the twentieth century, the Empire was a net liability to Britain, but it was nevertheless a major source of the kind of employment attractive to the governing class. The Second World War was a period in which the attractions of such employment began to dwindle and the composition of the governing class to undergo considerable alteration. As these two changes took hold, the wider popularity of the imperial idea started to evaporate. The British, as one politician put it over twenty years ago, no longer wanted to rule.

So, with many hiccups and occasional conflicts, there developed a trend of giving independence to every colony that wanted it – often before they were ready for it. Today this is another unfashionable notion, but the number of territories where the change from British rule to independence has been of real advantage to the mass of the people, as opposed to the new, indigenous governing class, should not be exaggerated. The upshot in the United States is only one of the exceptions to this proposition, but it is the exceptions that are conspicuous.

In the end, therefore, Britain was left with a handful of dependent territories she did not particularly want, either because their independence, however welcome to Britain, would not be tolerated by powerful neighbours – the Falklands, Gibraltar, Hong Kong – or because they were too small to manage on their own: Ascension Island or St. Helena.

No such general rules determined the different responses made by countries who either were, or who became, independent, to two key questions: would they stay in the Commonwealth and would they be monarchies or republics?

Of the original six self-governing dominions of 1926, for instance, Australia, Canada and New Zealand have not only remained in the Commonwealth, but acknowledge the Queen as their Sovereign. She is represented in each country by a Governor-General, but he is appointed on the advice of her ministers in Australia, Canada and New Zealand respectively and is expected to accept their advice just as, in the United Kingdom, the Queen accepts the advice of local ministers in that territory. It is not as Queen of the United Kingdom, but as Queen of Australia that the Queen is acknowledged in the latter country – for how much longer is uncertain. Ireland and South Africa, on the other hand, deserted both monarchy and the Commonwealth, while Newfoundland decided to join Canada.

Among the more newly independent Burma left the Commonwealth at once, wanting not even a shadow on her independence, as did other countries. Pakistan left the Commonwealth, as she left two alliances, because none of them would promise to support her against India, an early republic but always a vociferous member of the Commonwealth. Others started with the Queen as Sovereign, then became republics, but remained in the Commonwealth.

The result – as might be expected from anything in which the British have had a hand – is a legal and logical and constitutional nonsense. The Queen is Head of a Commonwealth mainly composed of republics, but with the odd indigenous monarchy, in a purely personal capacity. Her position is completely independent of any institution in Britain: executive, parliament, judiciary, electorate or any of the servants or rivals of the State. The title of Head of the Commonwealth confers no powers, though rather onerous responsibilities, but is subject to no very obvious control. This is a domain in which two of the Queen's traditional attributes are peculiarly appropriate. 'By the grace of God' is the most concise explanation I can think of for the Queen being Head of the Commonwealth at all. And 'Defender of the Faith' accurately describes her role.

There may be people more dedicated than the Queen to the idea of the Commonwealth, but, if so, they are anonymous. Her decision in 1983 to devote much of her traditional Christmas broadcast to a long discussion with Mrs Gandhi, then Indian Prime Minister, startled many insular viewers in Britain, but was wholly characteristic of the royal approach. In the same year there was political discussion in Britain of the extent to which the Queen had, or had not, been informed of the situation in Grenada before that island was invaded by the United States. Lingering local resentment of the attitude then adopted by Her Majesty's Ministers in the United Kingdom cast something of a shadow over the Queen's visit to Grenada in 1985.

In July 1986 the *Sunday Times* reported that the Queen regretted

Mrs Thatcher's refusal to comply with the wishes expressed by other Commonwealth Governments for sanctions against South Africa. The story attracted much over-excited comment from minor politicians and the media. And *The Times* published an almost unprecedented letter of rather carefully phrased denial from the Queen's Private Secretary. In this he declared it to be axiomatic that the Queen was 'bound to accept and act on the advice of her Ministers.' He was sensibly silent about the hypothetical contingency of the Queen receiving conflicting advice from her Ministers in 'other Realms'.

That is one of the less predictable results of turning the British Empire into the Commonwealth: it has reinforced the Queen's personal role in the dignified part of the British Constitution. The post-war governments, of both parties, who first attempted this delicate transformation had other motives.

These motives can be grouped in three broad categories, two of which were frankly sentimental. The first of these reflected the view of the old governing class: that the British Empire, for all its faults, had been a noble and civilising enterprise, making Britain the heir of Rome, and that its spirit should be perpetuated even if the realities of its power structure could no longer be maintained. That was a view which came even more naturally to Attlee – very much a member of the old governing class in spite of his leadership of the Labour Party – than it did to Churchill.

Among many of the new governing class, particularly on the Left, the old British Empire was more a cause for guilt than pride. For those imbued with such sentiments the emergence of the Commonwealth and the maintenance of the British connection offered the opportunity to make amends for past oppression and exploitation through cooperation and assistance on a new basis of equal friendship.

And mingled with both sentiments there were practical considerations of national interest. The emergence of a new Commonwealth, however independent its members might be of the mother country, held out the hope of retaining some of the markets, the enhanced diplomatic influence, the international prestige and even the military advantages the old Empire had conferred on a Britain whose intrinsic importance in the world was visibly shrinking.

Rather similar sentiments and calculations emerged in other ex-colonial powers, all of whom, from various motives and in different ways, endeavoured to retain a connection with their former colonies. The United States, for instance, have kept an important military base in the Philippines to this day.

If people throughout the world nowadays employ no national adjective, but talk about *the* Commonwealth (as, indeed, they talk about *the* Queen), Britain's lead in the post-colonial race had two main causes. The first was that the British Empire had been by far the largest and, if even only a majority of its members accepted continued association, was bound to produce the most conspicuous commonwealth. The second was that none of its members had actually expelled their British rulers by force of arms.

In many countries there had been unrest, civil disturbances, even riots and rebellions, but the final transfer of sovereignty had taken place by agreement. The departing British had left less hostility and resentment behind them than, for instance, the Dutch had left in Indonesia or the Portuguese in their African colonies or the French in Indochina. The relatively amicable nature of British withdrawal made the emergence of the Commonwealth possible.

Perhaps the most cynical compliment ever paid to the success of the concept came from Moscow, where the term 'socialist commonwealth' was coined to cover those countries which, in company with the Soviet Union, took action against Czechoslovakia in 1968.

The ritual of British retreat in good order from their colonies – the Union Jack lowered at sunset in the presence of a member of the Royal Family – also ensured that there was little ill-feeling in Britain itself: nothing to compare, for instance, with French reactions to the loss of Algeria.

Initially, therefore, the idea of the Commonwealth commanded a considerable consensus of support in Britain. Of course, there were always disputes about its practical implementation: the timing and conditions for the transfer of sovereignty in the different colonies, for instance. In the early years, however, the major impact on the British political system was the requirement imposed by the evolution of the Commonwealth for the maintenance of a greater defence effort and a higher degree of international involvement than was found necessary in comparable countries – Germany, for instance, or Japan.

Without the Commonwealth conscription would not have been so long maintained in Britain after the end of the Second World War (it was only abandoned in 1960) nor would it still be true that only 12 consecutive months have elapsed in the twentieth century without members of the British armed forces being killed or wounded in action. To begin with, these conflicts mostly arose from British attempts to delay, for good reasons or for bad, the acquisition of independence. For the last two decades the cause has mostly been assistance to independent members of the Commonwealth in maintaining their newly acquired independence. Ever since 1945, however, the Commonwealth has constituted, as did the Empire in many but not all peace-time periods, a net military burden on Britain. The compensating diplomatic advantages never matched initial expectations and have tended to decline. The once steadfast loyalty of Australia and New Zealand, who supported Britain even over Suez in 1956, is less reliable today. In the Falklands debate of November 1985 in the United Nations Britain did not get the Commonwealth backing that had once been so readily available on such issues as Gibraltar and Belize. The latter was one of the three countries voting for Britain. There might, of course, have been more if Mrs Thatcher had, during the previous month's Commonwealth Conference, manifested greater understanding of the sentiments of other members towards South Africa. Diplomatic influence depends on the principle of reciprocity. In Britain itself, however, the popularity of the Commonwealth idea has usually suffered from moralising, as it did, twenty years ago, from the lectures of such leaders as Nehru and Nkrumah.

There were also more tangible considerations, or so politicians believed. From 1945 onwards successive British governments thought they had three different options in the orientation of British trade with the rest of the world: a system of Commonwealth preference; a North Atlantic free trade area; and concentration on Europe as the main market for exports and source of imports. For reasons that were political rather than economic, Britain moved slowly and reluctantly from the first to the third.

This was not for want of economic arguments. The Commonwealth had more to offer than the traditional Australian wool, New Zealand lamb and Malayan tin and rubber. There was oil in Nigeria and in the states of the Persian Gulf (British protectorates as late as 1970); uranium in Australia; essential raw materials everywhere. And many of the countries that possessed them were very desirable markets indeed. Commonwealth preference, if it had been available, might have been better for Britain than becoming the dumping ground for duty-free consumer goods from Europe.

Commonwealth preference, however, was not available. None of the countries concerned had any objection to a preferential market in Britain for their own goods, but those that were independent or became independent regarded the right to shield their developing industries and to choose the source of their imports as part of their freedom. A Commonwealth Common Market was never a starter, only an illusion as durable as it was damaging.

The hope that the Commonwealth would provide Britain with captive markets sprang from the special circumstances of the years immediately after the Second World War. Many Commonwealth countries had accumulated large balances which they could only spend in Britain. The notion that this bonanza might persist discouraged lazy British manufacturers from modernising and becoming competitive. It also helped to delay Britain's entry to the European Economic Community until it was too late for this to do much good either to Britain or to Europe.

An incidental irony is that one of the sticking-points in the negotiation of British entry to the Community – and one of the few British successes in that arduous process – was the preservation of the British market for New Zealand lamb and butter. This was supported by all parties in Britain, where New Zealand had always enjoyed popular sympathy. And what happened? Today there is a surplus of British butter and, but for French political opposition, Britain would be a significant exporter of lamb. And New Zealand now restricts immigration from Britain.

It is in Britain itself, however, that immigration has been felt as the major political impact of the Commonwealth. In those far-off and distant days of 1947 and 1948, when the independence of India and Pakistan and Burma began the transformation of Empire into Commonwealth, nationality emerged as a serious problem. With important exceptions in the case of Protectorates and Mandated Territories and such like – nothing British has ever been tidy – people born in the British Empire were British subjects. Now India and Pakistan and Burma and, as could already be foreseen, other countries as well, would want to establish individual citizenships of their own. Moreover, not everybody who owed his British passport to his birth in Ottawa or Bangalore or Karachi or Rangoon while his father was on temporary service in those parts wanted to become a Canadian, Indian, Pakistani or Burmese citizen. So the British Nationality Act of 1948 invented a new kind of citizenship – of the United Kingdom and Colonies – and gave such people a year to choose.

But the Act did not abolish the concept of being a British subject. Instead it created a kind of dual nationality, a two tier system: British subject *and* citizen of wherever it was. Needless to say, this oversimplifies a complex statute.

This concept of dual nationality was not fully reciprocated elsewhere in the Commonwealth, but it was originally a very traditional, even a rather noble idea. *Civis Romanus sum* – I am a Roman citizen – had been a claim that any free man under the rule of Rome, whatever the country of his origin, might have cause to advance. A century before the British Nationality Act (1948) Palmerston, then British Foreign Secretary, had quoted that sentence. He did so to justify his use of extreme measures to uphold the right of a Gibraltarian, Don Pacifico, whose mixed ancestry had no Anglo-Saxon elements, to all the protection due to a citizen of the British Empire, the heir of Rome. That sentiment still prevailed in 1948: all British subjects should have equal rights throughout the Commonwealth and particularly in Britain, its source and centre.

What those who proclaimed such laudable sentiments did not then foresee was the ensuing influx of immigrants, in the exercise of the rights thus confirmed, into the British Isles. Of course, this was not simply the consequence of the British Nationality Act (1948). During the fifties and sixties, in the first phase of the great economic boom that lasted until 1970, all the industrialised countries attracted and imported relatively unskilled labour: Turks into Germany, Finns into Sweden, Algerians into France, Mexicans into the United States, Italians into Switzerland. Altogether over 11 million immigrant workers came to North West Europe. The nearly 2 million who came to Britain were different only because the immigrants had a legal right to come. They were not, as the Germans so tactfully described their immigrants, *Gastarbeiter* – guest workers. They were British subjects.

They came in such numbers – by 1961 the annual influx had reached 130 000 – that, even in this period of full employment, the number of jobs available for unskilled workers, many of whom lacked an adequate command of the English language, was no longer sufficient. Nor was the supply of cheap but decent housing. Too many of these immigrants had to put up with unemployment and squalid, overcrowded accommodation. These factors aggravated the often unfriendly welcome they encountered from the native inhabitants, particularly from those poor enough to regard the newcomers as direct competitors for houses and jobs.

A life half spent abroad, in five continents and many different countries, has sufficiently convinced me that nobody likes foreigners. But the British have, for centuries, been notorious for their chauvinism. 'It is easier', one refugee wrote in the reign of the first Elizabeth, 'to find flocks of white crows than one Englishman . . . who loves a foreigner'. And these immigrants were not only numerous – a million by the mid-sixties – but understandably inclined to settle in particular districts where they could continue their distinctive lifestyle. Above all, they were conspicuous, because they were coloured.

From 1962 onwards the growth of popular resentment among the indigenous British forced successive governments to pass a series of laws to restrict immigration, to narrow and vary the definition of British nationality and to deprive many of those who still held a British passport of their right to settle in this country.

Although many other members of the Commonwealth maintained or adopted restrictions of their own – Kenya, for instance, depriving Asians of citizenship and Uganda actually expelling all Asians, many of whom were then allowed to settle in Britain – something had been lost. British supporters of the Commonwealth ideal, more conspicuous in the governing class than in the mass of the population, recognised that their ideal had been gravely prejudiced by the legislative changes forced upon them. Nor did it help that worse things – or things at least as bad – had happened abroad. The worm was in the bud.

The unhappy growth of racialism in Britain, the impact on British society and the various expedients intended to mitigate some of the consequences may be left for later consideration. Here we need only note that problems connected with immigration have tarnished the image of the Commonwealth in British eyes as well as straining Britain's relations with other members. These had also suffered during the seventies from Britain's inability or reluctance to prevent the domination of Rhodesia by a white minority. That problem has since been solved (to whose lasting satisfaction remains to be seen), but years of constant criticism from other members of the Commonwealth did somewhat erode popular support in Britain for the institution. That process may continue, but now with South Africa as the cause.

Nevertheless, if there is one aspect of the Commonwealth even more remarkable than the rest, this is the survival of so strange an institution.

9 Parties and Factions

This chapter is concerned with the groups which people form in Britain for the specific purpose of influencing national politics and seeking at least a share of power. The resulting parties and factions may be regarded either as competing elements within the governing class or as rivals, in extreme cases enemies, of the State. If we ask to which category a particular party or faction belongs, the answer does not depend on our own prejudice alone. It may also vary from one year to another. Parties change and so does the nature of the State, to say nothing of the relationship between them.

The British Conservative Party, for instance, usually appear in the character of upholders of the State, particularly of 'law and order'. Yet proposals by the Liberal Government of Britain before the First World War to grant Home Rule to Ireland brought British Conservatives to the brink of armed rebellion. In 1912 the party's leader, Bonar Law, could 'imagine no length of resistance to which Ulster will go which I shall not be ready to support.' In April 1914, when another prominent Conservative, Sir Edward Carson, arranged the landing of 25 000 German rifles to arm the volunteers who were drilling in Ulster, the Cabinet considered prosecuting him for treason. In May 1915 Carson became a Cabinet Minister in a coalition government headed by the same Prime Minister – Asquith.

Circumstances do alter cases and everything in politics is relative. The descriptions that follow are thus of parties and factions, beginning with the strongest, as they appeared in the 1980s.

Most countries have a conservative party – the United States even have two – but the British are unusual in their readiness to call the party by its proper name. Elsewhere the favourite euphemism is Christian Democrat, but the Finns prefer to be entirely non-committal and call it the Coalition Party: an odd name for a party excluded for over twenty years from successive coalition governments. The Canadians, true to their English ancestry, have boldly opted for a formal contradiction in terms: Progressive Conservative.

All these parties have as their objectives the preservation of the capitalist system, the defence of property rights and the avoidance of disturbing change in the social order. The British Conservative Party, however, has many strands and has undergone considerable evolution during the present century. Among the Conservative Members of

Parliament elected in 1983 there were few of the country gentlemen so long so prominent in the party's ranks. Lawyers and businessmen predominated and only 5 per cent described themselves as farmers. On the other hand, 71 per cent had a university education and 70 per cent had attended private, fee-paying schools. Most Conservative Members of Parliament must, therefore, have come from reasonably prosperous families. Only 1 per cent had been manual workers.

How has such a party managed to win 6 of the 12 general elections, all conducted on the basis of universal suffrage, since 1945? The answer seems to be that social class has less influence on the way that people vote than on the way that parties choose their candidates. In 1983, for instance, less than 50 per cent of manual workers voted for the Labour Party and 31 per cent of trade unionists voted Conservative. One of many reasons for this cross-class voting seems to have been that workers who had bought their own cars and their own homes often regarded the Conservatives as more likely to preserve them in the continued enjoyment of these privileges. In 1985 63 per cent of British homes were owned by their occupiers (in 1950 only 30 per cent) and successive Conservative governments have gained many voters by the measures they have taken to make it easier for working people to buy their own homes and thus to acquire a personal stake in the existing social system. So politicians believe, but some theorists are sceptical (Heath *et al.* 1985).

Conversely, areas of high unemployment and widespread poverty, whether in certain inner cities or in the regions dominated by old and now declining industries, tended to vote Labour. The electoral strength of the Conservative Party was concentrated in the relatively prosperous southern half of the country.

Of course, the Conservatives (or Tories, as they are often called) had more to offer the voters than just the maintenance of the capitalist system and property rights. Their prospectus included patriotism (particularly appealing after victory in the Falklands War); law and order (popular in an era of violence); the claim to greater managerial skill in government; a leader commanding respect if not always liking; and a radical programme for curing Britain's economic disease. They were greatly assisted in that election by the internecine quarrels of the Labour Party and by the continuing unpopularity of that party's paymasters: the trade unions. An increased majority for a government that had seen unemployment more than double was still something of a surprise.

If the Conservative Party differs from its foreign counterparts mainly in its remarkable record of electoral success, the Labour Party is a more curious and specifically British phenomenon. Founded early in the century by the trade unions to provide them with a parliamentary voice, it was not originally an avowedly socialist, let alone Marxist party. It came forward to champion the cause of the working class, but derived its inspiration more from the dissenting churches and the instincts of solidarity than from any clearly formulated ideology. Labour inherited the task and much of the support of the Liberal Party, whose earlier enthusiasm for social progress seemed to have exhausted itself by the time the First World War began.

The success of the Labour Party in winning votes soon attracted more ideological socialists, who had made little headway on their own. Between the wars, therefore, the party became, as Harold Wilson (party leader from 1963 to 1976) later described it, a broad church. The party embraced all shades of opinion from near-communism to views that, on all subjects except trade union membership and working-class solidarity, differed little from Conservative attitudes. Ernest Bevin, the self-educated trade union leader who became Foreign Secretary in 1945, maintained a foreign policy that was perhaps more assertive, nationalist and anti-Russian (certainly the last) than a Conservative Foreign Secretary would have considered politically prudent. Of course, Bevin, unlike some members of the party, was also a strong supporter of all the innovations – nationalisation and the welfare state – which the Labour Government carried through at home.

From 1945 to 1979 it may reasonably be argued that the Labour leadership, in and out of office, did not seek to destroy the capitalist system, but to reform it, to humanise it and to make it serve the interests of the people as a whole. How much success this had is arguable, but it did not satisfy the more left-wing, ideologically committed members of the party. The majority shared Wilson's view that the Labour Party should be a party of government, which meant accepting both the compromises needed to get elected and the compromises needed to run the country.

This majority was eroded by the world economic depression of the seventies. As it became obvious that Labour governments from 1974 to 1979 were neither meeting the aspirations of their supporters nor maintaining even the earlier rate of economic and social progress, the dissatisfaction and the influence of the left wing of the party steadily increased. They demanded policies that were specifically socialist, denounced acquiescence in international constraints, rejected as a valid objective the kind of political power that could only be achieved and retained by compromise, insisted on the need for irreversible changes in British society (the word 'irreversible' even got into the Labour Party manifesto in 1974) and wanted measures to ensure that activists in the constituency parties and in the trade unions could exercise effective control over the decisions of Labour members of parliament and Labour ministers.

The resulting division inside the party between those who sought power within the existing system and those for whom only power to change the system was worth having gave rise to noisy and much publicised disputes. These damaged the image of the party in the eyes of the electorate, contributed to the loss of the 1979 election and prompted the departure of a number of right-wing Labour MPs to found a new party – the Social Democrats.

These quarrels were still raging at the time of the 1983 election, when the programme offered to voters – withdrawal from the European Community; a non-nuclear defence policy (including a refusal to allow American cruise missiles in Britain); more nationalisation; a massive rise in public spending and, perhaps the most damaging of all, the right of local authorities to repurchase houses sold to private owners – was visibly not supported by some of the party's leading figures. One of them, Peter Shore, understandably called it the longest suicide note in history. Under an elderly compromise leader, Michael Foot, with a gift for tripping over himself, the party fared disastrously.

It has, however, often been argued that the real weakness of the Labour Party stems from the erosion of its class base through a shift in the pattern of employment. One recent book (Heath *et al.* 1985) suggests that the working class of manual wage-labourers has shrunk from 47 per cent of the electorate in 1964 to 34 per cent in 1983. Terms of employment (such as relative security or independence) are said to have greater political influence than income levels. Non-manual workers, the self-employed and supervisors are thus less likely than the real working class to vote Labour.

It may also be significant that many of the more extreme and committed socialists come from the ranks of the educated. 53 per cent of Labour MPs elected in 1983 had a university education, though only 14 per cent had attended fee-paying schools. Labour actually had more university teachers in the House of Commons than did the Conservatives, but the fact that 33 per cent of Labour MPs had been manual workers still indicated a major social difference in the representation of the two parties. It also shows, incidentally, that entry to the British governing class is more accessible than is sometimes supposed, even if its composition does not reflect that of the population as a whole.

The Liberal Party has undergone many vicissitudes since its zenith in 1906, when it provided a reforming government with 49 per cent of the votes and 400 MPs. After the First World War a fatal split led to the party being squeezed into a shrinking minority between Conservatives and Labour. By the end of the Second World War the Liberals were a fringe party, unable even to contest most seats, accustomed to losing deposits, securing only a handful of MPs. Efforts to modernise their image as the decayed heirs to a vanished tradition attracted mainly the discontented, and sometimes eccentric, members of the middle-class. The Liberals became – and this is their weakness – a party of dissent and of opposition. They survived – and they have some potential for the future – because of the increasing disaffection of the electorate from both the Conservatives and Labour.

Since 1945 the share of the total vote taken by the two major parties has declined from 90 per cent to 70 per cent. One of the causes has been the big increase in the number of Liberal candidates. At the general election of February 1974 the Liberals got 14 seats, a minor triumph after managing only single figures in 6 out of the previous 7 elections. In a House of Commons where no party could command a majority, Liberal votes became important, though not decisive. They refused support to the defeated Conservative leader and, at a later stage, extended it to Labour.

Although the Liberals gained little by their choice, the experience encouraged them to hope that they might one day so decisively enjoy the balance of power as to be able to impose ministers and policies on a coalition government. These hopes (a little dashed by the loss of votes and seats in 1979) were much increased by the emergence in 1981 of the Social Democratic Party (initially comprising defectors from the Labour Party) and the subsequent formation of an electoral alliance between the two parties.

In 1983, however, this Alliance secured 26 per cent of the votes, but only 3.5 per cent of the seats in the House of Commons. Their first objective, therefore, must be to get enough votes next time (probably over 30 per cent would be needed) to produce sufficient MPs to hold a real balance of power. Only then could they insist, as the price of their support, on the introduction of proportional representation. This seems to be the Liberal objective, though David Owen, the leader of the Social Democrats, qualified it in November 1985 by suggesting that the first step should be a referendum. But proportional representation, however this is achieved, does appear essential if either party is to have much future as a serious contender for power.

At present, so public opinion polls suggest, the Alliance parties face a dilemma. More people would vote for them if only they believed their votes would not be wasted, but could actually bring the Alliance to power. But what, except the attainment of power, can persuade the electorate that power is attainable?

The main assets of the Alliance are two leaders – David Steel for the Liberals and David Owen for the Social Democrats – who perform well on television and attract the many electors discontented with both the major parties. Their weakness, apart from the bias of the electoral system, is their failure to agree on a clear, coherent and convincing political stance. Everybody knows what they are against – the evils of adversary politics – and many people sympathise. There is less understanding of what they are for. In the second half of 1986 the Alliance seemed to be losing some support because of much publicised differences on defence policy, particularly on the emotive issue of nuclear weapons.

Those voting for both parties, incidentally, were spread across all classes. The members actually elected resembled the Conservatives in their educational background, but there was only one businessman and no manual workers at all.

These four, Conservative, Labour and the Alliance of Liberals and Social Democrats are the parties with a serious prospect of achieving at least a share of power within the present political system. Table 9.1 presents a rough statistical comparison.

Table 9.1   Statistical comparison of the main political parties

Party	Conservative	Labour	Liberal	Soc-Dem
Membership	1 200 000	323 292	105 000	55 000
			Alliance	
Votes 1983	13 012 602	8 457 124	7 780 587	
% of vote	43.5	28.3	26.1	
% of MPs	61.1	32.1	3.5	
MPs in 1983	396	209	18	7

If Northern Ireland is reserved for separate and later consideration, all other parties and factions received in 1983 a total of only 655 667 votes and most of these went to the nationalist parties in Scotland and Wales.

Before turning to these lesser parties, it is worth considering how the big four choose their leaders. The secular trend, of course, has been away from the old idea that the Monarch personally selected the politician most likely to command a majority in the House of Commons and invited him to form a government. Macmillan, in 1957, was the last Prime Minister to be chosen in that way. He would himself have preferred to preserve this aspect of the prerogative, but the soundings taken in the Conservative Party while Macmillan was in hospital in 1963 were so elaborate as to constitute almost a straw vote for his successor, Alec Douglas-Home. In 1964, when Wilson became Prime Minister, he had previously been elected, as have all his successors in that office, leader of the party by a majority of its members in the House of Commons.

Today, however, the Conservatives are alone in retaining so narrow an electorate. Only in the Social Democratic Party is the leader elected by a direct, secret ballot of all the members, but this is also the only party with a national membership rather than one organised regionally or by constituencies. The Liberals allow their constituency associations the decisive voice, but the Labour Party give them 30 per cent, another 30 per cent going to Labour MPs and 40 per cent to the block votes of the trade unions.

The Social Democratic preference for 'one member, one vote', as opposed to the indirect election favoured by other parties, is also reflected in the choice of parliamentary candidates. There, however, the impact is diminished, because the decision that a particular seat should be fought on behalf of the Alliance by either a Liberal or a Social Democrat is not reached by democratic process, but through hard bargaining between the leaders of the two parties. This is not always the case. In 1986 the prospective parliamentary candidate for the Alliance Party for Cambridge City was chosen by a postal ballot of the constituency members of both parties.

The Social Democrats thus constitute only a partial, though a significant exception to the general rule that this particular gateway to the governing class is guarded by an elite of committed activists. It will be interesting to see how far the present practice, particularly in the Conservative and Labour parties, will be affected by the example of the trade unions, which are beginning, in response to legislation of Conservative origin, to ballot all their members on issues previously decided by activists.

Of the lesser parties the nationalists deserve most attention. The Welsh *Plaid Cymru* seems to have spoilt its chances by excessive identification with the Welsh language, spoken by only a small minority of the people of Wales. It is a fringe party, likely to go on electing one or two members of parliament but no more, its national credibility effectively destroyed by the results of the 1979 referendum in Wales. The rise and fall of the Scottish National Party is more of a puzzle. In the seventies its band-waggon seemed to be rolling and many Scots jumped on board. After the 1979 referendum they jumped off again, leaving the party with only 12 per cent of Scottish votes in 1983 and two MPs. Scotland being a Labour stronghold, further erosion of that party's vote might again give the nationalists a chance.

Then there are the factions, both splinter groups within the established parties and those outside organisations neither directly represented in the House of Commons nor with much hope of electing a member under their own names. They may conveniently be considered in connection with the parties already mentioned.

Within the mainstream of Conservative politics the most important faction comprises those, sometimes described by Margaret Thatcher as 'wets', who lack enthusiasm for the full stringency of her economic policy. They would prefer a higher priority for the reduction of unemployment, for investment in Britain and for the maintenance of the Welfare State, even at the cost of higher government expenditure and taxation. They are well represented in the House of Commons, have not been entirely eliminated from the Cabinet and obtain occasional victories.

Among the factions of the right are those favouring more drastic restrictions on trade unions and coloured immigration, together with the restoration of capital punishment. Some of them are alleged to sympathise with the frankly racialist, not to say fascist attitudes of the National Front, an organisation attracting a handful of votes but with little hope of electing an MP. Perhaps of equal importance are the various groups, ostensibly academic or professional, which contribute to the doctrines or the funds of the Conservative Party.

Within the Labour Party there is an entire spectrum of factions, usually grouped under three labels (which roughly reflect increasing readiness to change the constitution to achieve socialism): moderate, soft left and hard left. The moderates have been losing ground for many years, but have rallied a little since the 1983 election, which the hard, and even the soft left are widely supposed to have lost for the Labour Party. At present, therefore, the party is dominated by a loose alliance between soft left and moderates, the leader, Neil Kinnock, being generally regarded as soft left.

The principal faction (as opposed to individual members of the Labour Party) of the hard left is the Militant Tendency, a Trotskyist organisation which has successfully infiltrated the Labour Party; dominates the Young Socialists; has two members in the House of Commons and more sympathisers; enjoys influence among constituency activists and in local government. Unlike moderates or soft left, the Militant Tendency aims at a degree of political, social and constitutional change which can fairly be described as revolutionary. The present leaders of the Labour Party, particularly embarrassed by the reckless way the Militants exploited their dominating position on the Liverpool City Council, have repeatedly tried to exclude them from the Party. This has proved difficult, because the Militants, for all their disciplined cohesion, regularly deny that they constitute a separate faction. And the old slogan of 'no enemies on the left' still has its appeal.

During 1986 the Labour leadership also sought to limit the embarrassment caused by other splinter groups of the hard left. These are numerous, much smaller than the Militant Tendency (which is said to have 7000 members), often variously Trotskyist, much given to quarrelling among themselves and inclined to support a wide range of unpopular causes, such as the Irish Republican Army (IRA), the Palestine Liberation Organisation (PLO) and positive discrimination in favour of coloured minorities. They too have sometimes acquired positions of influence in local government, but in national politics they have mainly become sticks with which to beat the Labour Party.

The orthodox Communist Party of Great Britain has suffered from its links with the Soviet Union ever since that country ceased to be a war-time ally. No declared Communist has been elected to the House of Commons since 1945 and both party membership and electoral votes have declined almost without interruption. Bearing in mind that Communists manage to get elected even in that temple of capitalism, Switzerland, this curious phenomenon is presumably due to a combination of British chauvinism and the effects of the electoral system.

In 1983 35 Communist candidates could muster a total of only 12 000 votes, the worst result yet. The Communist Party is squeezed between Labour and the Trotskyists, who reject Stalinism and the right to leadership of the Communist Party of the Soviet Union. Orthodox communism has largely lost its former attraction for students and the young. Its remaining strength is in the trade unions. Not only do some important unions, the National Union of Mineworkers, for instance, have Communists among their leaders, but cooperation with the rest of the Left seems to encounter fewer difficulties there than in the purely political field. In general Communist influence has undergone less decline than party membership.

An organisation covering a broad political spectrum, though with little Conservative support, is the Campaign for Nuclear Disarmament. This calls, with varying degrees of emphasis, for the renunciation of British nuclear weapons, the withdrawal of all American nuclear weapons from the British Isles, the adoption of a non-nuclear defence policy and, at the very least, severe restrictions on the development of nuclear power. The organisers claimed 110 000 paid-up members in 1985 (more than either the Liberal or the Social Democratic Party) and many times more sympathisers.

Public opinion polls suggest not only that support is strongest on the Left, but that this varies with the particular cause being advocated. The withdrawal of American cruise missiles from British bases or scrapping plans to buy expensive Trident submarine-launched ballistic missiles from the United States command wider sympathy than the unilateral renunciation of *all* British nuclear weapons. This last grates on the instinctive nationalism of the electorate.

Nuclear disarmament has many sympathisers in the Liberal Party and is a source of disagreement between them and the Social Democrats. To the outsider, indeed, the Liberal Party often seems a mere collection of factions: for and against alliance with the Social Democrats; preferring either a lonely purity or else the chance of a share of power, though uncertain whether Labour or Conservatives would be most acceptable; variously preoccupied with nuclear disarmament, ecology, free trade, homosexual rights, civil liberties, devolution and local democracy; unanimous only on the need for proportional representation.

The Social Democrats have their differences, but, as a new party with a strong leader and a programme emphasising consensus, have fewer factions or outside affiliations. Their greatest problem, as with the Liberals, is likely to come when the choice of a leader for the Alliance can no longer be postponed.

The Nationalist parties embrace many different views: independence or some lesser autonomy; nationalism alone or combined with social change; the peaceful or the violent struggle. There is, or used to be, a Scottish Workers' Revolutionary Party and a sabotage organisation called Scots Against War as well as a few Welsh nationalists addicted to violence.

Britain shares with other industrialised democracies the characteristic distemper of late twentieth-century civilisation: a rash of minor terrorist organisations and politically motivated criminals. Native groups (unlike those with foreign, particularly Irish, roots) tend to be more vicious than dangerous and Britain suffers less than many countries in Western Europe, where only Finland has so far been immune.

Pressure groups are of much greater political importance, far more numerous and also more various. Manufacturers or financiers or lawyers or doctors may combine to promote their special interests as do workers in their trade unions. Many ethnic minorities have some kind of organised representation. Other groups bring together people concerned with some single issue: the rights of women, 'gay liberation', organic farming, the prevention of cruelty to animals. Some pressure groups can expect greater sympathy from one political party (or faction) than another, but most try to influence anyone able to assist their cause. The outlet which pressure groups provide for the views of their members is essentially an alternative to that offered by the political parties, though such groups may naturally operate within parties as well as at cross purposes to strictly political alignments.

If Britain differs at all in this respect from comparable countries, it is perhaps because special interests are less politicised. There are many conservationists, but the Green Party has yet to make a significant impact on national politics. Some of the obstacles to small parties have been mentioned, but money is not yet a major problem. More is spent nowadays on politics in Britain than in 1950, when the Prime Minister, Attlee, undertook electioneering journeys in his private car with a notoriously bad driver, his wife. But even in 1983 the central expenditure of the three main parties amounted to £8 million, a trivial total by American standards.

Very little of the expenditure of political parties in Britain, in contrast to the practice in some other countries, is funded by the State, which only began in recent years to contribute anything beyond the salary of the Leader of the Opposition. The Social Democrats derive a larger share of their income from members' subscriptions than do the other main parties, but they and the Liberals have also needed wealthy donors. The Labour Party admit to getting most of their money from the trade unions and the more reticent Conservatives probably get much of theirs from limited companies.

All British political parties experience recurrent financial difficulties, sometimes overcome by rather dubious methods when in power. The former Liberal Prime Minister, Lloyd George, was more blatant and unscrupulous than anyone else in conferring peerages and other honours on contributors to party funds. The practice has not been unknown to recent Conservative and Labour governments, but has been on a much smaller scale. No major political party nowadays asks would-be parliamentary candidates how much they are prepared to contribute to party funds and the American practice of choosing ambassadors from among the politically generous has never been imitated in Britain.

Parties are nevertheless not popular in Britain. This was true even before it became fashionable to blame all the ills of the nation on the practice of adversary politics. Most people probably agreed with Winston Churchill that 'putting party before country' was a grave charge to bring against a Prime Minister. The target for this indictment, incidentally, was one of Churchill's predecessors in that office: Stanley Baldwin. A party as the supreme magnet for loyalty is a foreign notion scarcely to be found in Britain except in the ranks of the Hard Left and among a minority of professional politicians.

Whatever their other faults, the political parties do provide a valuable, perhaps even an essential mechanism for the operation of representative democracy. Without parties it is conceivable that the pace and scope of necessary change in Britain would have been greater, more salutary and, above all, more consequent. It might also have been less peaceful. During the twentieth century Great Britain has been one of only three countries in Europe where authority within the state has always been transferred by constitutional process and never by force. The other two (not counting Andorra, Gibraltar, Liechtenstein, Malta etc.) are Sweden and Switzerland. Luck may have been as much the cause as system, but the existence of political parties made a contribution. They moderated the struggle to control the State, refreshed and renewed the composition of the governing class, limited the abuse of power.

It is regrettable that the growth of political parties in Britain, indeed, the extension of representative democracy, should have coincided, since about 1867, with national decline, but most European experience in this period suggests the British people may have escaped worse fates. Even today neither revolution nor *coup d'état* deserve serious consideration among the potential threats to their future.

10 Divisions on Constitutional Issues

Both practitioners and analysts might question whether 'constitutional issues' deserved much prominence in any discussion of today's divisions in British politics. Such issues are seldom debated in the House of Commons, nor do they often figure among the questions with which public opinion pollsters try to sample the views of the electorate. Once the idea of devolution had withered in the 1979 referendum, proposals for constitutional change lost the place they had briefly occupied in the centre of the political stage. They became academic or, what was almost as bad, the hobby-horse of the Alliance, which needed proportional representation to enjoy any lasting prospect of power.

There is some force in this objection. Constitutional change matters more to the Alliance than to other parties and they do spend more time talking about it: not just proportional representation, but also decentralisation, freedom of information, a bill of rights and other ideas as well. The Alliance are not alone. The Labour Party are forever talking about abolishing the House of Lords and, when in opposition, favour a Freedom of Information Act. Conservatives have in the past flirted with devolution and, until Margaret Thatcher stamped on the idea, even with proportional representation.

In February 1987, however, no British political party supported the eminently constitutional Human Rights Bill introduced into the House of Commons after being passed by the House of Lords. This proposal to incorporate in British Law the European Convention on Human Rights was a Private Member's Bill sponsored by a Member of Parliament in his individual capacity.

But, given the peculiar ways in which the British constitution evolves, there is much more to this question than the handful of proposals which political parties have publicly backed and which they have labelled as projects for constitutional change. In the past much has been altered by accident. There began to be prime ministers in Britain because King George I had insufficient command of the English language to preside at cabinet meetings. Even more changes have been the unintended result of decisions which, at the time, were not envisaged as having any constitutional character.

When writing, nearly twenty years later, of his decision in 1916 to establish a Cabinet Secretariat, it obviously did not occur to David Lloyd George that, when he became Prime Minister, he had made an important constitutional innovation. He saw himself as taking a practical step to improve administrative efficiency at a time when the demands of war made efficiency imperative. The consequences were first glimpsed in 1922 and have only been fully revealed in the reminiscences of Cabinet Ministers during the last couple of decades. It is thus necessary to consider the present scope for real constitutional change as well as for that which its advocates choose to call by that name.

The two are not always easy to distinguish. If the wider implications of change are sometimes overlooked, it is also true that politicians often like to dignify their disputes by declaring them to involve 'constitutional issues'. That was the case with the quarrel among Conservative Ministers in the winter of 1985–6 over the future of the Westland Aircraft Company. By some accounts it concerned the nature of cabinet government as much as the manufacture of helicopters.

Although the idea of constitutional change has most appeal for politicians in opposition, it would be wrong to regard the electorate as entirely indifferent. Thinking about the constitution as such may come more naturally to voters in the United States or other countries with written constitutions. There the actual text is often available in the kind of reference book – the equivalent of Whitaker's Almanac – to be found on quite modest bookshelves. It is harder for British voters to discover the contents of their own constitution and they tend to express their views only in answer to specific questions. In April 1985 a public opinion poll did so and came up with some interesting figures. Only 55 per cent of those who answered thought the British political system was working well and from 46 per cent to 57 per cent favoured some kind of constitutional change: freedom of information or more independence for local government or proportional representation or a bill of rights.

These are obviously constitutional issues, but there are others. Behind all the cut and thrust of current debate, inside Parliament and beyond, lurk two questions unlikely ever to receive a final answer: what should be the nature and purpose of the State and how may the people best seek to influence their rulers? One of the reasons why they remain unanswered is that the questions are seldom properly formulated.

For instance Mrs Thatcher has often claimed, both as her objective and as her achievement, a reduction in the previous dominance of the State in individual lives. What she meant by that seems to have been a decrease in the relative importance of transfer payments. People should pay less tax and themselves choose how to spend their increased income, instead of relying on the State to meet all their requirements for accommodation, medical care, education, financial assistance in emergencies or pensions when they were too old to work. Services should be provided by private firms, whose competition would increase their efficiency, to those who chose to pay for them.

Economically this attempted alteration in the role of the State has been somewhat frustrated by a massive rise in unemployment. More people now have to rely on the State for their subsistence, while those still earning must contribute a larger share to the State. There have also been social repercussions requiring later examination. But to present even the original objective as a reduction in the dominance of the State, as constitutional rather than political, is surely to take an unduly narrow view.

If we consider the policies followed under the Thatcher administration towards local government or the trades unions or the universities, on public order or the choice between freedom of information and official secrecy, we may well argue that both objective and achievement have been to reinforce the control exercised in many fields by central government: that is the State. How far there has been a decline in the political freedom of the individual *vis-à-vis* the State is again a subject for later discussion, but this is quite as material to the argument as any enlargement of economic options.

Of course, the way in which the Thatcher government conduct the business of the State is vigorously criticised by their opponents. But these critics rely on arguments of economic expediency or social priorities, on attacking specific actions rather than broad principles. Criticism has a political character; it is more partisan than constitutional. It is not open to the Labour Party, for instance, to adapt the words of the eighteenth-century resolution passed by the House of Commons and to declare that 'the influence of the State has increased, is increasing and ought to be diminished.' Diminishing the influence of the State is the last thing they want – as long as they retain the hope of eventually controlling the State.

Constitutional issues in Britain are thus latent rather than actual, implicit in much of the current conflict and debate, more often discussed by academics and in the intellectual back rooms of politics than in the House of Commons or the media. They are nevertheless important and for two main reasons.

The first is that there is no longer a sufficient consensus in Britain about the true nature of our unwritten constitution or about the validity of such constraints as it has previously been assumed to impose on the emergence or the operation of executive power in the State.

The second is that challenges to the authority of the State are becoming more frequent, more popular and more violent.

Naturally the constitutional differences and the violent challenges of British seventeenth-century history make today's problems look like a teddy bears' picnic. Even in good Queen Victoria's golden days the Duke of Wellington assumed command of the troops holding the Thames bridges against a revolutionary demonstration threatening to invade the Houses of Parliament. The clerks of the Foreign Office were issued with muskets and the future Emperor Napoleon III, then an exile in London, enlisted as a special constable. Nothing like that has happened in Britain during my lifetime, though opposition to the Vietnam war caused President Johnson to bring an armoured division into Washington and, after the Paris riots of May 1968, President de Gaulle flew off to Germany to discover what support he could count on from French military units there.

Nevertheless we do have what Harold Macmillan once splendidly described as 'little local difficulties.' Poor Mrs Thatcher has had to cope with disturbing strikes; with the violent urban riots of 1980 and 1981; with what can only be called the Scargill insurrection of 1984 to 1985; and still more urban riots in 1985. One of the bitterest blows, for a party dedicated to law and order, must have been the 1982 Home Office report that fear of crime in Britain's inner cities had reached American levels. These more spectacular manifestations of unrest were supplemented by numerous ostensibly peaceful demonstrations, marches, sit-downs, occupations and the sustained blockade, by protesting women, of American nuclear bases.

Popular dissension found disturbing echoes within the actual citadel of the State. Not only did numerous civil servants go on strike, admittedly from mercenary and thus understandable motives, but others betrayed secrets for political reasons and attracted the sympathy of sections of the media as well as of those politicians who derived advantage from the disclosures. The rivals of the State, as I have earlier described them, are more numerous, more active and, above all, more violent than they used to be. Mrs Thatcher, in one of the more excitable remarks that occasionally escape her, has even gone so far as to talk about 'enemies within'.

Of course, it is not easy for the agents of the State to discriminate between enemies – those criminals prepared to kill, maim and intimidate people, as well as wrecking their homes and belongings – and rivals, who merely seek to cause embarrassment and inconvenience because they believe the State to be deaf to reasonable argument. A policeman accustomed to a rain of bricks, bottles, steel bolts and fire bombs may not always show sufficient tenderness when dragging away people whose protest has been confined to lying down in the middle of the street. The extent and variety of challenges to the State has inevitably generated a more repressive response. The police have been reinforced, given extra pay, provided with riot equipment and trained in tactics that are, in intention, defensive and necessary for defence, but which can sometimes seem provocative, even aggressive or over-reactive. The State is one of those wicked animals which, when attacked, defends itself.

Nevertheless, if at least some popular perceptions of the State have altered, causing it to be seen as less concerned to help the unfortunate than to encourage the successful, to be concentrating on efficiency at the expense of equality, to be no longer just bossily paternalist but actually repressive, then this is not merely a political argument. Potentially it is also constitutional, because acceptance of the State as we have known it has rested in part on the assumption that anything wrong with the policies and conduct of the State could and would change with the next change of government. In the fifties and sixties such changes regularly occurred and were accepted as zig-zags rather than radical and lasting departures from the framework of consensus.

Today that period is regarded by all parties as one of economic failure: Labour blames compromise with capitalism; the Conservatives the shackles then imposed on enterprise; the Alliance the abrupt changes of course with every change of government. Naturally the remedies they favour differ widely, but all of them want to introduce lasting change. Labour are most open about this, calling for irreversible change and decisive moves towards a socialist society. The Conservatives avoid this kind of language, but many of their practical measures are so designed as to frustrate attempts at socialist change: the abolition of exchange controls, the compulsory sale of council houses at low prices to their tenants; special inducements to persuade workers to acquire shares in denationalised enterprises. As for the Alliance, their advocacy of proportional representation is not entirely selfish: they also hope to prevent the future dominance of the State by the radicals of either major party, virtually to make consensus compulsory.

If Labour come to power or if the Alliance win an effective share of power, overt constitutional change will be inevitable if either party is to achieve its objectives. The Labour Party, for instance, can scarcely pursue its 'New Economic Strategy' – essentially one of economic nationalism – without colliding with the European Economic Community, whose rules and regulations are now effectively components of the British constitution. Other frequently expressed objectives – such as correcting the capitalist bias of the Civil Service, education, the judiciary and media – have significant constitutional implications. So does the idea of bringing the police under democratic control or the notion that a Labour government would be bound to carry out the policy laid down by the Labour Party Conference, who could punish any deviations by appointing a new leader of the party, thus in effect dismissing the Prime Minister.

Of course, there is no telling what real changes the Labour Party would actually feel able to propose with any hope of electoral success or how important the outcome would be in practice. All kinds of scenario have been envisaged from mere apparent change – abolition of the House of Lords and of titles and decorations, for instance – to the real transformation of Britain into some kind of socialist society. All we need note is that one of the major parties in Britain has in recent years put forward a programme calling for significant constitutional change. Both Benn and the Militant Tendency, needless to say, have gone further.

The Alliance demand for proportional representation may seem more modest, but the prospect it opens up of coalition governments, perhaps even short-lived and unstable governments, could have profound repercussions. So could some of their ideas about devolution or choosing the Prime Minister in a general election.

Nor can it even be said that continued Conservative government would rule out the prospect of constitutional change. That might be the case if the Conservatives were more successful than now seems likely in restoring the British economy. But the present combination of massive and rising unemployment, declining social services and increasing privileges for the successful can scarcely be prolonged indefinitely without subjecting the social fabric to severe strain. Under such pressures the real character of the British constitution might change more than its appearance.

One issue of potential significance is the manner in which ordinary people will seek to influence their rulers. In principle, a great many perfectly proper and constitutional methods are available for the pursuit of individual grievances. Most members of parliament, for instance, spend quite a lot of time trying to help individual constituents seeking their assistance. If the Member has no success with Ministers, he can invoke the aid of the Parliamentary Commissioner for Administration, a kind of equivalent to the Scandinavian Ombudsman. There are citizens advice bureaux, there are consumer protection agencies and there is a rather rudimentary system of free legal advice. Business firms and the rich can employ political consultants with members of parliament on their pay-roll, a privilege also enjoyed by other groups and organisations. Trade unions will often help their members and if you are poor enough, you can get free legal aid and go to court. Newspapers and the media frequently give powerful ventilation to newsworthy grievances. All this is much better than it used to be.

The difficulty comes when your grievance concerns not bad administration or breaches of the law, but what you consider to be bad policies or bad laws. It is significant, for instance, that the British Ombudsman is not allowed to question policy decisions. Judges usually disclaim any right to interfere with a Minister's reasonable exercise of the discretion given him by Parliament. There are, admittedly, now new loop-holes available: appeal to the European Court of Justice against some British law or policy that conflicts with Community law, or to the Council of Europe against violations of the European Convention on Human Rights. Such expedients are neither cheap nor in common use.

On the whole, once your grievance is general rather than particular, against law or policy rather than their detailed application, then your only resort is to the political process. And politicians are partisans: they normally support their party. The most you can usually expect is an assurance from an opposition politician that, if you support his party and if his party wins the next election, something will be done about it some time. Meanwhile, perhaps, he will undertake to ask a question or to mention it in the next convenient debate.

Such assurances, their inherent uncertainty and the prospect of long delay do not always satisfy ordinary citizens. Those who follow the news are aware of other and quicker ways of ventilating their views and forwarding their cause. They combine with others to make themselves a public nuisance. Historically this is not a novel approach and it can be matched today in most Western countries: American demonstrators against the Vietnam War or for civil rights; Germans blockading nuclear power stations; lorry drivers closing the Alpine passes; sit-downs everywhere and French farmers against almost everything, particularly British lamb. What is disquieting about this process is threefold: it is proliferating; the extent of public inconvenience and the level of violence acceptable to the organisers are increasing; and it calls in question the whole concept of representative democracy.

It is this last aspect that ominously raises constitutional issues. Naturally it has often been necessary, in all eras and countries, for exceptional grievances to be manifested in ways that violate constitutional norms. Many changes are so unwelcome to the governing class that they must be forced rather than persuaded to accept them. During the nineteenth century, for instance, the British governing class were rather smug about their ability to recognise when popular agitation made constitutional reform essential, contrasting this experience with the revolutions and civil wars of other countries. Today, however, changes in the political system, whether in Britain or elsewhere, do not seem to be keeping pace with the increased incidence of political disaffection.

Pressures for constitutional change in Britain are local symptoms of a fairly widespread condition. Few of the industrialised democracies today are free from outbreaks of politically motivated violence or other manifestations of mass dissent. Most states have had to increase their repressive apparatus in response. These symptoms, which naturally vary in character and intensity from one country and one year to another, may have common causes in popular dissatisfaction with existing political systems and with the representative democracy – the indirect expression of the popular will – that is supposed to be their common principle.

But there is another international aspect to be considered. Britain today belongs to more multilateral organisations and is a signatory of more multilateral treaties than ever before. There are also bilateral understandings and arrangements, some of them secret, particularly with the United States. The nexus of international obligations thus created may not, in pure theory, create any kind of constraint on constitutional change: what one parliament has accepted, another parliament can repudiate.

In practice there is a real constraint and of a somewhat paradoxical kind. As already mentioned, a left-wing Labour government might find it hard to pursue their New Economic Strategy while remaining a member of the European Economic Community. Either this membership must be accepted as restraining political change or that change must be extended from the political to the constitutional. But the likely international reactions to Britain's leaving the Community, to say nothing of the necessary infractions of the rules of GATT and the IMF and similar organisations and agreements would drive such a Labour government to the swift adoption of measures to prevent the flight of capital, to restrict imports and generally to assume stringent control of the economy. The end result might be the partial withdrawal of Britain from the international capitalist system and very considerable restrictions on the right of British capitalists to control the use of their capital.

This is a paradoxical constraint. It offers to the opponents of the Labour Party useful arguments to dissuade electors from supporting that party. The threat it implies could strengthen the hand of Labour moderates against their militants. To the Hard Left, however, the thought of the damage such policies might do to the position of capitalism in Britain is a positive incentive. Moreover, if they can once begin the process, they can rely on the chauvinistic British reaction to any foreign action to help them persuade doubters that they might as well be hung for a sheep as a lamb.

The international constraints that discourage moderate changes of policy might thus, if they fail in this purpose, actually encourage changes more extreme and frankly constitutional. In British politics there is still an alienation effect: an instinctive hostility to anything done by foreigners.

Argue as one may, constitutional change is not a salient feature of the political agenda in Britain. The Conservatives do not want it; the Labour Party are anxious not to frighten the electors by talking about it; the Alliance must win a lot more seats in an election fought on other issues before their demands for proportional representation and other changes will be taken seriously. But deep in the holds of the Ship of State some chemicals are smouldering: the implications of the programmes of the political parties; the precarious state of the economy; restlessness and disaffection in some sections of the people. Unless the Conservatives are unexpectedly successful in getting the economy going again, a change of wind could produce a constitutional fire.

11 Divisions on Economic and Social Policy

More than any others, economic and social issues divide the parties in Britain and engage the attention of voters. This happens in most countries, because economic and social issues involve more people and come closer home to them as personal choices than do considerations of foreign policy, defence policy, civil liberties or other slightly remote problems of government. When such problems cease to be remote, as has sometimes happened in Britain and is true today of some other countries, people usually have more to complain of.

British preoccupation with bread and butter issues is understandable, because, for the last hundred years, the British economy has been a perpetual problem. Of course, it has not been so dramatic a problem as it was in 1929 in the United States, when banks closed all over the country; falling bodies made it hazardous to stroll on Wall Street and, as I can myself remember, sad beggars shuffled from house to house in the prosperous suburbs. Nor was there ever a million pound note, nor did British shoppers use wheelbarrows to transport their money, as happened in Germany at much the same period. The thirties in Britain were harsh for many Britons, but the nation as a whole did not come near enough to collapse to persuade the majority to rethink their attitude to economic management. One consequence was regrettable.

The British people only began to realise there was something fundamentally wrong about twenty years ago. Before there were so many external causes to blame for Britain's economic difficulties. It is important to remember, for instance, that the two world wars were economically damaging for Britain, whereas the First World War and, to a lesser extent, the Second was very profitable to the United States. These excuses were running out by the sixties, when it became obvious that European countries, having suffered even more than we did in the Second World War, were nevertheless making a better and faster recovery. That was when at least the politicians began to see the economic debate as involving a search for new and more radical solutions.

Ten years later it was obvious that their first ideas had failed: Wilson's dream, when he was Prime Minister in the sixties, of a new technological revolution in Britain; the decision to join the European Economic Community; Heath's initial emphasis in 1970 on private enterprise and competition; the attempt by the Labour Government that followed him in 1974 to enlist the trade unions as partners. What was more, the collapse after 1970 of the long, post-war boom in the Western world was reinforced by the impact of the 1973 energy crisis. These international echoes helped to bring British failures home to British electors. In the first quarter of a century after the Second World War real incomes in Britain had doubled and unemployment had averaged less than 2 per cent. The British people as a whole were better off than they had ever been and could afford to ignore politicians croaking that the French and the Germans and the Swedes and the Swiss were doing still better.

There was even a rather strong line in British complacency about the quality of life in Britain being so much more agreeable than anything available in more harshly competitive countries.

This is not – and I have spent half my life abroad – entirely nonsense even today. In June 1986 *The Times* pointed out that the French, who enjoy a significantly higher income per head, were twice as likely to commit suicide as the English and Welsh. They also consumed double the amount of alcohol and tranquillisers. Americans, Austrians, Germans and Japanese were others who surpassed the English and Welsh in their pursuit of both the profit motive and the death wish.

A society cannot, of course, be judged by the single test of its suicide rate. Ulster has the lowest in the United Kingdom. Perhaps an anecdote would help. On Christmas Eve of 1984 my wife, who was suffering from flu and bronchitis, was visited at home by her National Health Service doctor. We paid him nothing and he received nothing extra for visiting us at home on such a day. I told this story to an international audience and asked whether any of them could offer an example from their own country that was at all comparable. No one could.

- Nevertheless, during the seventies, trains got dirtier, streets had more holes, schools fewer books, the waiting lists for optional operations got longer. Money was saved by delay and neglect. Strikes became more frequent. From 1973 to 1979 there was an absolute decline both in British industrial production and in employment. Something was clearly wrong. In 1979, therefore, the electorate were more open to radical proposals than they had been earlier. The only surprising feature was that this opportunity for radicalism was exploited not by the Left – final crisis of an expiring capitalism – but by the Right.

The explanation, of course, was the dismal record of the Labour governments in office from 1974 to 1979: 24 per cent inflation, forced to crawl for help to the International Monetary Fund (who imposed humiliating terms) in 1976; the famous 'winter of discontent' in 1978–9, when the public service unions reacted to the income policies attempted by the government with a series of strikes that deprived hospital patients of laundry, casualties of ambulances, ordinary citizens of rubbish collection and even the dead of burial. Orthodox Labour had little left to tempt the voters.

The Left Wing, admittedly, offered their New Economic Strategy. This was, to put it crudely, for Britain to spend her way out of depression by greatly increasing investment and govermental control of the economy. The idea that British capitalists should be compelled to invest their money at home rather than abroad was, as it remains, in itself not unattractive. Nor was the notion that unemployment (which had reached 1 300 000) could be cut by reducing the length of the working week, thus compelling employers to hire more people to do the same amount of work.

When the Left Wing went on to argue that inflation could be avoided by controlling prices, but leaving wages free to rise, many voters began to smell a rat. And, although the electorate were ready to listen to arguments for leaving the European Economic Community, they were sensitive to the counter-attack mounted by the Conservatives. These insisted that the Left Wing programme would mean a siege economy and the return of rationing; that leaving the Community would also mean leaving NATO and would end with Britain as a People's Republic.

In 1979, therefore, many voters thought the policies of the orthodox Left, as these had been applied by Labour governments during the previous five years, had failed. They were daunted by the political implications of the more extreme New Economic Strategy and they were irritated by the inability of the Labour Party to agree among themselves. Monetarism – the Conservative prescription – was at least new – most people wanted something new – and sufficiently incomprehensible to be less alarming than the alternatives on offer.

In the late seventies monetarism still seemed a magic formula. For years the bogey of successive British governments had been the way wages rose faster than output, producing inflation at home and deficits abroad. Attempts at the direct control of wages had all foundered, sooner or later, on the rock of trade union power. The Labour Party had no more success in trying for a Social Contract with the unions than the Conservatives in their bid to control wages and strikes by law. The public had to suffer the increasingly disagreeable consequences.

Now, so the Conservatives promised, the government would no longer attempt to control wages: it would simply reduce the money supply. All but the most profitable firms would be unable to raise wages and, if faced with a strike, would go bankrupt, thus depriving strikers of their jobs. The lesson would soon be learned by the unions, who would stop striking. Wages, inflation and the balance of payments would thus all be painlessly controlled by the magic of monetarism, which would be further assisted by reducing taxation and government expenditure.

Of course, it didn't work out quite like that. No economic policy ever does. And, to be fair, Mrs Thatcher and her supporters had always said they would need at least two full parliaments to restore the British economy to health. Nearly seven years later a Conservative Chancellor of the Exchequer was still complaining (in March 1986) that the pay of British workers was rising faster than their productivity or than the wages of their foreign competitors. How far the Conservatives have got on the economic road they outlined in 1979 is one of the most controversial issues in British politics today.

It is controversial in two ways. For the ordinary voter the answer depends to an unusual extent on his personal circumstances. For those politicians who profess to be concerned with the national interest as a whole, the answer is unusually dependent on value judgements.

If the ordinary voter, for instance, lives in the southern half of the country, has a good job in an expanding industry, owns his house and is both ambitious and confident about his own future and that of his family, he may think Mrs Thatcher has made some progress. Inflation is down, but his wages are up; he is probably paying less direct tax and is pleased that central government are keeping tight control over the rates levied by local government. He may be one of the million voters enabled by the Conservative government to buy at bargain prices the houses they had previously been renting. He may even think that the poor and the unemployed are at least partly to blame for their own misfortunes.

The picture looks different in the north of the country, home of so many old and declining industries, and in some decaying inner cities throughout the country. The more than 3 million unemployed receive less immediate help and see less prospect of a job in the future. The prosperous may welcome cuts in expensive social services, but the unemployed rely on those services for a bare and often rather hopeless existence. In the more fortunate South voters may accept government assurances that present austerity will bring future prosperity: the unemployed know, even if they do not remember who said it, that in the long run we shall all be dead.

This sharp division of attitude is also reflected, in more sophisticated form, among politicians. What seems to be lacking is any satisfactory basis for an objective judgement. In January 1985, for instance, Professor Skidelsky, the economic historian, began an article with the words: 'After five years of Mrs Thatcher's rule it is still extraordinarily difficult to say whether her government has reversed or accelerated the decline of Britain.'

That remains true, for the relevant statistics are conflicting and, because they are not always calculated on the same basis, sometimes hard to compare. At the beginning of 1986, for instance, over 14 per cent of the British work force were unemployed. This was a worse ratio than in Canada, France, Germany, Italy, Japan or the United States. It was, however, *better* than in Belgium, the Irish Republic, the Netherlands or Spain. It was three times worse than it had been in Britain ten years earlier. On the other hand, the deficits on the balance of payments encountered in the late seventies were replaced in the early eighties by repeated surpluses, though 1986 again brought a deficit. Manufacturing output in 1985 was 5.5 per cent lower than in 1979, but productivity (reflecting the rise in unemployment) had significantly improved. Inflation, which rose alarmingly in the early years of the Thatcher administration, was nevertheless lower, at 5.7 per cent in 1985, than the 13.4 per cent of 1979.

Naturally it is possible – and politicians do it every day – to pick on certain years for comparison and to single out particular statistics so as to create the impression that the economic policies of the Thatcher government have been either a brilliant success or an abject failure. And any comparison is capable of different interpretations. Conservatives are proud of the improvement in Britain's balance of payments; the Opposition attribute it to the reckless squandering of North Sea oil.

In March 1986 the Conservative Chancellor of the Exchequer boasted that Britain's net overseas assets had risen from £12 billion in 1979 to almost £90 billion in 1985. His failure to ensure that this money was invested at home was deplored by the Opposition.

The statistics for such countries as Japan or West Germany display trends that are almost uniform. The revelation, in March 1986, that Japan National Railways had debts of £140 billion must have excited the envy of British Rail, but was otherwise an exception that only helped to prove the rule. The economic success of these two countries cannot be disputed and the only argument concerns the social and political costs. In Britain such economists as Professor Sidney Pollard discern a consistently downward trend, but their arguments are often attacked by politicians anxious to rescue the reputation of governments of their own party and to pin more of the blame on their rivals.

Much of the debate in Britain, moreover, is concerned with relative rates of progress. Unemployment is one of the few economic indicators to register absolute deterioration year after year. Those in work enjoy higher real earnings for shorter hours. They eat better, have more comfortable houses, take longer holidays, can expect to live to a greater age. For them it is still true – though less conspicuously than when Lord Stockton said so in 1957 – that 'you've never had it so good'. The unemployed, on the other hand, are not merely more numerous than at any time since 1945. They are also worse off, relatively to those in work, than in earlier years.

These comparisons over time – of the experience of the young with that of their parents – are probably of greater political importance than the equally striking contrasts between economic achievements in Britain and in other countries of North Western Europe. What has happened over the years in Britain is felt; being overtaken by the Europeans is something that only a small minority, continental package holidays notwithstanding, have really hoisted in.

Moreover, although both politicians and, if we may believe the public opinion polls, electors are agreed in according priority to economic issues, what they are really talking about is what used to be called political economy. Statistics are assessed, proposals weighed and progress measured by standards that are highly political and vary from one party to another.

Conservatives consider it important not only that inflation is down, but that business profits are up; that the rate of increase in government expenditure is slowing; that state enterprises are being sold to the private sector; that top rates of income tax have been reduced, foreign exchange controls lifted and indirect taxation increased. All these changes, they believe, are good in themselves and will eventually be reflected in even better statistics. In the Conservative view what matters is not the size of the British economy, either in terms of output or in those of employment, but whether or not it is profitable. Only profits can fertilise growth and increase remunerative employment.

The Labour Party disagree with all of that and the Alliance with much of it. To them the British economy exists to employ British people and to provide them with the goods and services they need. Profitability is a secondary issue and can even be a harmful concept, if it can only be attained by running the economy at a level too low to provide full employment, to retain essential industries and to replace the national infrastructure. The Labour Party, in particular, advocate a large increase in expenditure by the State to reduce unemployment and lend fresh vigour to the economy.

This is a greatly over-simplified account of party differences on economic policy. One of the more curious complications is a tendency for the Left to strike more nationalistic attitudes than the Right. Conservatives nowadays see merit in toughening the British economy by exposure to those harsh winds of international competition from which Labour, and to a lesser extent the Alliance, would like to shield the 'wee, sleekit, cow'ring, tim'rous beastie'. It is not an economic judgement, if there is such a thing, but an ideological, even an emotional reaction, which causes politicians (some of them on Conservative back benches) to dislike foreign ownership of industries located in Britain. The reasons for regarding Japanese proprietors as a lesser evil than American have nothing to do with economics and would take too long to explain.

Conservative Ministers, on the other hand, have become as eager as any nineteenth-century Liberal to reduce governmental interference in what they consider the self-regulating activities of the British economy. The low profile they now favour in this field is in sharp contrast to their active concern with law and order; with controlling the trade unions, local government and the bureaucracy; with defence and security.

The Labour Party have always favoured a tighter grip on the economy by the State, even if they have been prepared, when in opposition, to contemplate some relaxation in other sectors of the national existence. Where the two parties seem to converge is in their distrust of the European Economic Community, seen by the Conservatives as unduly interventionist, by Labour as hopelessly committed to capitalism. But, in matters economic, Labour has taken over the nationalism which once characterised the Conservatives. The Alliance, claiming to be both tough and tender, want the best of all possible worlds. They positively favour British cooperation in

Community policies and, at home, seek a middle way between the laissez-faire Mrs Thatcher rather surprisingly borrowed from the heirs of Gladstone and the fluctuating approaches to fuller state control which the variable fortunes and internal divisions of the Labour Party seem to prescribe.

In the running economic debate that takes up so much political time in Britain, Labour are most vulnerable to charges that their return to power would lead, through increased inflation, taxation and trade union dominance, to the reimposition of so much state control as to create a siege economy for Britain. The Conservatives are accused of tolerating needlessly high unemployment, of favouring foreign capital and the indigenous rich, of squandering North Sea oil and, in the words of Lord Stockton, of 'selling the family silver' by their practice of denationalising state undertakings. The Alliance have so far exposed fewer targets for attack, but are criticised (particularly by the Conservatives) for advocating economic policies tried in the sixties and seventies and then found wanting. None of the parties can point to a past record of such success as to lend much plausibility to their prescriptions for the future – least of all for the time, which may well come in the next decade, when there is no longer enough oil left in the North Sea to sustain Britain's balance of international payments.

It is, of course, their social consequences that sharpen these otherwise uncertain economic arguments. For a quarter of a century, from 1945 to 1970, successive governments regarded the maintenance of full employment as the touchstone of British economic policy. Only in the seventies did unemployment, long kept under half a million, start the steady climb which has accelerated so sharply under Mrs Thatcher.

The Conservative government have preferred to regard this as an economic phenomenon, the consequence both of world depression and of the previous over-manning of unprofitable British industries. Although they have tried to mitigate the impact of unemployment by training programmes and similar palliatives, they have consistently refused to jeopardise other economic objectives by trying to create jobs. Their reluctance has been sharply criticised, not only by Labour and the Alliance, but by two former Conservative Prime Ministers: Lord Stockton and Edward Heath.

In February 1986 the Confederation of British Industry (which represents the employers) urged the government to spend a billion pounds on job creation, and similar recommendations have come from other Conservative supporters. Public opinion polls usually record majorities believing that the Government could and should do more. *The Times*, a consistent supporter of Mrs Thatcher's economic strategy, qualified their praise of the 1986 Budget with the comment: 'there is still something half-hearted about the Government's approach to job creation.'

Politically it may not matter much whether the advocates of increased government intervention are right to believe that this could significantly reduce unemployment without damaging side-effects (by increasing inflation, for instance). If they succeed in labelling the Thatcher Government as 'uncaring' – and many of the recent reforms and economies in the administration of social security fit that picture – this could have an important influence on the outcome of the next general election. Economic efficiency is probably less attractive to the electorate than its social fruits and these have recently acquired a bitter taste. The miners' strike was followed by a teachers' strike that disrupted the education of many British children. Riots in Handsworth and Tottenham reiterated the alarming message of Brixton and Bristol. The problems of ailing industries were insensitively handled. Unemployment rose remorselessly.

What is more the constant emphasis given by the Thatcher Government to the need to reduce public expenditure has coarsened their public image. Mainly because of unemployment, more of the national income has been spent by the State than under the previous Labour Government. But a combination of insensitive rhetoric and cheese-paring has deprived the Conservatives of any credit for their spending. Instead – naturally with the active assistance of the Opposition – all the deficiencies of the health service or the social services, every riot or strike or death from hypothermia, are blamed on the harsh choices made by Ministers.

Economic disagreements often end in statistics that everybody interprets differently, many do not believe and few understand. The social consequences are regularly depicted on the television screens. One of them, as people of various political views might agree, is a touch of political disaffection, even alienation. This has not been confined to crumbling inner cities or embittered miners' villages.

In January 1985 Oxford, which is quite a reputable university, refused by a large majority to follow the traditional practice of awarding an honorary degree to any Prime Minister who had graduated from Oxford. They did so because they considered Margaret Thatcher's policies inimical to education and science in Britain. Doubtless other factors – the pay and conditions of service of university lecturers, for instance – were involved, but the vote showed how widespread and how sharply felt political divisions had become. In September 1986 Harvard were reported as having done the same to President Reagan.

A week, let us remember, is a long time in politics. By the time the Thatcher Government decide to face the voters in 1987, or have to face the voters in 1988, some of the more traumatic effects of their economic and social policies may have been alleviated. Reducing inflation to 3 per cent was a transitory achievement in 1986, but the rate should still be much lower at the next election than it was in 1979. It would be an unusual and unlucky government that could not produce some kind of budgetary bonanza on the eve of the polls.

So far, however, there are certain aspects of economic and social conditions in Britain – particularly those related to unemployment – where the Conservative Government have yet to regain what were once regarded as the intolerable levels of 1979. These prompted the British electorate to break with the consensus politics of earlier decades and to vote for radical change. In 1983, so it can be argued, the success of the Thatcher Government in the Falklands War, together with the obvious disunity and incompetence of the Labour opposition, persuaded voters to overlook the uncomfortable fact that most of them were no better off after four years of Conservative government than they had been in 1979. Next time they might be less indulgent and be offered more of an alternative.

If Mrs Thatcher cannot satisfy the electorate – and it seems she still has some way to go – that she has really improved their circumstances and their prospects, the choice may lie between a return to consensus, perhaps entailing success for the Alliance in a coalition government, and a swing to the Left. So far Margaret Thatcher's best allies have been leading members of the Labour Party, but, if they ever got their act together and if the Government's run of bad luck were to continue, the swing might go rather far. The present administration have been pursuing policies which involve significant social risks, but which have yet to produce a wholly convincing economic dividend.

12 Divisions on Foreign and Defence Policy

Defence and foreign affairs are as much debated in Britain as economic and social policy, but the arguments exchanged have a rather different character. Most politicians are less committed by party membership, ideology or social origin to a particular view. Naturally there is a marked difference between the attitudes and assumptions on the right wing of the Conservative Party and those to be found on the left wing of the Labour Party, but there is a good deal of common ground in the middle.

Moreover, when governments of either party have taken controversial decisions about defence or foreign policy, these have not always reflected conventional notions of their ideological commitments. No Labour Government, for instance, defied the United States as Eden did over Indochina in 1954 or Suez in 1956: on the first occasion as a Conservative Foreign Secretary, on the second as a Conservative Prime Minister. The Labour Government of 1974 made a conscious effort to smooth away the prickliness they thought their Conservative predecessors had needlessly imparted to Anglo-American relations.

It was a Labour Government that took the unprecedented decision to maintain conscription even after the Second World War had ended and a Conservative administration that later abolished it. Attlee's Labour Government secretly decided Britain should have her own nuclear weapons; subsequent Conservative governments were criticised by Labour in opposition for keeping them; the Labour governments of Wilson and Callaghan, in the seventies, spent billions on their further development. In the eighties the Thatcher governments found more money for defence and struck a sharper note in international discussions, but made no changes in foreign and defence policy that matched the radicalism of their new approach at home.

The unfolding pattern of international events has done more to modify British defence and foreign policy than the programmes of British political parties. Debate has always been vigorous, but much of it has taken place within political parties rather than between them. The enduring division has not been between Left and Right, but more

Divisions on Foreign and Defence Policy

between insiders and outsiders. Within the Labour leadership, for instance, it is primarily experience of ministerial office that accounts for the difference between the views of Denis Healey and Neil Kinnock.

An older and more general source of disagreement, as well as an important reason for its persistence, was the difficulty experienced by the British people in adapting themselves to their drastically diminished importance in the post-war world. This difficulty has often been criticised by people who emerged from the Second World War stronger than ever, such as the Americans; or whose self-esteem had been surgically reduced by defeat and enemy occupation, such as most of the Europeans; or who had abandoned their imperial pretensions over a century earlier, such as the Swedes.

To appreciate the magnitude of the British psychological problem, it is necessary to remember that Britain and her Empire were belligerents longer than anyone else; had, for a particularly critical year, been the only significant enemy of an all-conquering Germany; and had emerged at the end as the notional equal of the Soviet Union and the United States in the triumvirate of the victors. The British Isles were more battered than ever before, but a quarter of the globe still acknowledged a British monarch and British forces had never been so widely dispersed. The British people knew their exertions had impoverished them, but regarded this as a transitory phenomenon. A perhaps excusable pride prevented them from realising that their power was still more ephemeral.

Of course, there was some contraction even in those early years: withdrawal from India and Pakistan and Burma and Palestine; reductions in British overseas responsibilities – for Greece, for instance; even sharper reduction in the size and geographical dispersion of British armed forces. Of course, the process never went far or fast enough. Nobody ever told the British people that they were now too poor to be a Great Power, should abandon their overseas commitments and concentrate on the restoration of their economic strength.

Every withdrawal was treated as an isolated and regrettable incident. The saga of the Overseas Base was the longest running farce in recent British history: first it was to be in Palestine; then in the Egyptian Canal Zone; then in Cyprus; then in Mombassa; then in Aden. The Chiefs of Staff with, I regret to say, some assistance from the Foreign Office, always had admirable reasons for spending millions of pounds, as well as the lives of British soldiers, on each of these fantasies in turn. None of them were ever any use and it is hard to imagine the circumstances in which they could have been. Our allies were often as keen as we were on these chimeras. In the late sixties both Americans and Australians tried to persuade the British Government to hang on to Singapore – a base that had proved a useless liability in the Second World War.

Part of the trouble sprang from the pragmatic British tradition of tackling problems as and when they arose, on their individual merits, not as part of a preconceived plan. The bureaucracy were trained to be responsive and the politicians usually found foreign affairs an uncongenial field for major new initiatives or grand designs. Votes could seldom be won in foreign affairs, though they could easily be lost if an initiative misfired or even if mere bad luck led to a setback. Moreover, any forward-looking, comprehensive foreign policy in the fifties and sixties would have had to be one of avowed contraction: lowering Britain's profile to match the relative decline in her resources.

This was not what anybody wanted to hear. An isolated withdrawal might pass muster as the necessary response to exceptional circumstances. Otherwise the British wanted continuity and, if that appearance could be maintained – preferably enlivened by a touch of drama in gesture or rhetoric – would cheerfully put up with acts of lunacy: indefinitely prolonging the stay of British forces in Germany; proclaiming Britain's frontier to be on the Himalayas; refusing either to cede or to defend the Falklands.

This makes it sound as if there had been a consensus after all. What common ground actually existed – small and sensible minorities apart – was that of ignorance and of inability to take a general and dispassionate view of the imbalance between British resources and British commitments. The individual problems tended to be hotly disputed.

That was true, for instance, of each phase of our long, gradual, often painful withdrawal from Empire. The Conservatives usually wanted to delay withdrawal and the Labour Party to hasten it. Once withdrawal had taken place, however, their attitudes sometimes reversed themselves, with the Labour Party more eager than the Conservatives to provide economic or even military support for some newly independent country.

Looking back over the last forty years, however, it is easy to get these problems out of perspective. Perhaps there was too much nostalgia in Britain for vanished grandeur, for the afterglow of

Divisions on Foreign and Defence Policy 121

Empire; too many sentimental illusions about the ability and willingness of the emerging Commonwealth still to make us look larger than life. We would be better off today if we had jettisoned the Great Power image much earlier and concentrated on a much more radical economic reconstruction. Yet, when you think what other countries got up to – the Dutch fighting a losing battle in Indonesia for over three years; the French in Indochina for eight and then repeating the experience in Algeria; the Portuguese holding out even longer in Africa; the Americans breaking every record with twenty wasted years in Vietnam – you begin to think that perhaps the British didn't do so badly after all. Not every colonial campaign led to dinner at Buckingham Palace for the once rebel leader, but we seldom made quite such a large and expensive mess of things as some other people.

Where we really did slip up, of course, was in failing to realise how important the European Economic Community was going to become, thus missing the chance to get in on the ground floor. There were many reasons for this: illusions of grandeur in the Conservative Party; the fear of the Labour Party that the Community was a capitalist conspiracy to prevent socialism in Britain and break up the Commonwealth; a general distrust in Britain of the founder members. We easily forget that in the fifties even German economic progress had not yet overtaken British; that France and Italy were not merely poorer than we were, but had weak and unstable governments; that those Nordic and neutral countries later gathered by Britain into the rival European Free Trade Area were more congenial and respectable and also looked a better political and economic bet. And, at the time when the British were less thoroughly disillusioned by their own governments, it was important that a Free Trade Area involved no encroachment on sovereignty.

By the time British politicians realised their error, of course, it was too late: General de Gaulle had come to power in France and, little though he personally cared for the Community, was determined that French dominance of that institution should not be challenged by a Britain too closely committed to the United States.

That commitment, shared language and traditions apart, was essentially a matter of defence. The military tail wagged the diplomatic dog for most of the post-war decades in Britain, particularly after 1956. The Suez fiasco demonstrated the inability of Britain and France to make a significant intervention in international affairs without at least the acquiescence of the United States. The two countries reacted differently: France, thanks mainly to General de Gaulle, devoting herself to the acquisition of the material basis for independence; Britain renouncing independence in order to maintain, at less expense, its economic and military appearance.

At the beginning of the seventies there was a possibility of altering this stance. The leaders of both British parties now favoured membership of the European Economic Community. General de Gaulle was no longer an obstacle. Heath, the new Conservative Prime Minister, wanted both a European Foreign Policy and a European Defence Policy. To achieve this, as he demonstrated in 1973, he was willing to risk American displeasure by rejecting the crack of the whip manifested in Kissinger's notorious Year of Europe: an attempt to coordinate European policy under American leadership.

Movement towards a federal Europe would probably have been aborted in any case by the autumn oil crisis of 1973, but it had really failed earlier. President Pompidou, distrustful as de Gaulle but less imaginative and courageous, did not respond to Heath's overtures. Heath himself ran into trouble at home from the trade unions; the bureaucracy were against it and his Labour successors were both suspicious of the Community and determined to reorientate British policy towards Washington.

Ever since the turning-point of 1956 the British attempt to maintain Great Power status had increasingly depended on military cooperation and assistance from the United States. The price that had to be paid was political dependence. Only Heath briefly and unsuccessfully envisaged an alternative.

Because this dependence could not formally be admitted, it tended to undermine consensus on foreign and defence policy and to foster conflict between insiders and outsiders. From 1964 onwards participation in government convinced Labour Ministers that Britain could not afford to quarrel with the United States over Vietnam, misguided though American policies seemed – and eventually proved – to be. Many of their supporters in the House of Commons and in the country denounced this prudence as cynical or cowardly. It is, of course, often the duty of Ministers to be both, but British politicians of all parties still find it difficult to admit to the electorate just how limited Britain's options really are.

As a result each new government has a difficult initial period: Ministers must convince the bureacracy that the voters have expressed new aspirations; the bureaucracy must explain that the world and Britain's place in it have also changed since Ministers were last in office. As a general rule, after some initial fireworks on issues of secondary importance – Rhodesia or Chile or South Africa or whatever – the new government settle down to accepting what has gradually evolved, in the give and take of years, as established British policy. The bureaucracy will be united, and thoroughly plausible, in expounding the horrors to be expected from significant change.

That is another reason why the 1975 referendum on British membership of the European Economic Community was such a shock. It was not merely unconstitutional: it was unprecedented. A policy, laboriously hammered into agreement during 15 years of bitter controversy at home and abroad, was suddenly being subjected to a popular vote. Many bureaucrats only survived because they steadfastly refused to believe it was happening – a belief in which they were, of course, confirmed by the outcome of the vote.

So long a discussion of the events of earlier years was unavoidable, because present British divisions on foreign and defence policy cannot be understood without a backward glance at the curious process which got us where we are today. That had three main elements: the long retreat from the global responsibilities of a Great Power; belated entry to Europe; growing dependence on the United States.

The first element has really ceased to be a political issue. The Conservative Government that came to power in 1970 had deplored, when it was arranged by their Labour predecessors, British withdrawal from the Persian Gulf and from Singapore. They tried to set up a token Five Power Defence Agreement centred on Singapore. Mrs Thatcher has been content with the symbolism of extended naval cruises and managed to make a sensible arrangement to wriggle out of Hong Kong. The Falklands War was no exception to the general desire for contraction, merely a reminder that the British must still be ranked among those wicked animals who sometimes defend themselves when attacked. If General Galtieri's most passionate purpose in life had been to keep the British flag flying at Port Stanley, he could scarcely have chosen a better method – expensive though it was. What the British should do now is, of course, a more controversial question.

Only Argentina, Guatemala and the strategic requirements of the United States – at Diego Garcia, for instance – keep the British extra-European role in existence. Left to themselves the British, and others concerned, would be more than happy to allow the Commonwealth to remain in the afterglow of an indefinitely prolonged imperial sunset, a purely dignified aspect both of the constitution and of the international scene.

Membership of the European Economic Community was always,

for Britain, a fall-back position. Unfortunately, the fifteen years (1958–72) which elapsed before Britain took the plunge had made the conditions of entry much harder for Britain. The original six members had become increasingly set in their ways, ever less disposed to make concessions to Britain, whose economic decline made it obvious that she now needed the Community more than the Community needed her. Even the British Government's economists could not promise any immediate advantage from entry to offset the certainty of large and increasing contributions from British public funds to those of the Community. The case for entry really rested on a trinity of intangibles. It would have a dynamic effect on British industry, generating new investment and reversing the long process of relative decline. It would make Britain part of a Third Force in the world, destined to grow not only in economic importance, but also in political unity and, eventually, even in military significance. And, whatever the cost of membership, Britain would be worse off outside than in.

Only the last of these arguments still survives today. After a dozen years the magic of the new dynamism has yet to transform the British economy. Hopes of Europe as the world's third Great Power withered and died in the *sauve-qui-peut* which followed Arab use of the oil weapon in 1973. As the individual governments stampeded in panic-stricken quest of private deals with the producers, abandoning the Netherlands (victim of a total embargo) to be rescued by the international oil companies, the idea of Community solidarity sank to the level of tokenism at which it has remained.

Naturally successive British governments helped to prick the bubble. But the result has been to thin the ranks of the Community's committed supporters in Britain and to dilute their enthusiasm. The Conservatives (but for a handful of nationalists on the right of the Party) accept Britain's membership of the Community as a fact and have been energetically trying to reduce the cost to Britain by arguing that contributions should be directly related to national wealth. The forceful tactics employed by Mrs Thatcher were not popular in the other capitals of the Community, but have done her no harm at home.

Although, in terms of British politics, the Conservatives are reckoned as supporters of the Community, their attitude might sometimes be described as making the best of a bad job. There is also a tinge of ideological suspicion. To a British government endeavouring to reduce government expenditure, to liberate private enterprise and to diminish the role of the state in the national economy, the Community's bureaucrats seem over-mighty and too inclined to

Divisions on Foreign and Defence Policy 125

extravagant interventions. Where the Community is concerned Margaret Thatcher sees herself as Boadicea, defending national sovereignty against the Treaty of Rome.

The Labour Party are no less distrustful, resenting Community membership as an obstacle to the pursuit of socialist policies in Britain. Although only the left wing of the Party actually advocate withdrawal, there is less support for the Community in the Labour Party than in the Conservative and more suspicion. If withdrawal is not official party policy, this is because so many members are daunted by the sheer practical difficulty of the operation; fearful that, at least in the short run, it would only aggravate Britain's economic problems; and sure that so drastic a prospect would alarm the electorate and lose votes.

Among politicians the Alliance are perhaps the warmest supporters of the Community: partly because most of them have not been disillusioned by experience in government; partly because of internationalist sympathies; partly because the Community seems to reflect their own preference for the Middle Way.

Perhaps the staunchest allies in Britain of the Community are the bureaucracy. Not only are British officials always conscious of the objections to disturbing what already exists, but the very intricacy of the Community, the multiplicity of the channels of communication it has generated among the member states, all the rules and regulations and arrangements that only the experts understand: all this has strengthened the position of the bureaucracy at a time when it is unpopular with the radicals of both Left and Right and much in need of all the foreign support it can get.

For those who believe public opinion polls, about 48 per cent of the people usually support British membership of the European Economic Community. This is a higher ratio than the proportion of British voters prepared to take part in the direct election of British members of the European Parliament: 32.6 per cent in 1984 compared to the 72.7 per cent who voted in the purely British general election of 1983. The low turnout may reflect a British perception that the European Parliament has less influence than the British Government over such powerful bodies as the Council of Ministers of the European Economic Community or the Commission.

Similar considerations apply to the North Atlantic Treaty Organisation (NATO), which now constitutes the core, not merely of British defence policy, but of British foreign policy as well. This is a remarkable example of that familiar political phenomenon: the displacement of ends by means. Originally NATO was a means: a military alliance intended to promote British independence and national survival. It was meant to overcome the post-war demoralisation of a devastated Western Europe. Otherwise, so it seemed at the time, European countries might fall under Soviet domination, as did Czechoslovakia in 1948, without even a shot being fired.

It should really have been a temporary expedient. A series of historical accidents made NATO an instance of the old saying: nothing lasts so long as the provisional. Soviet behaviour in Stalin's last years was alarming; the French insisted on Anglo-American insurance against the dangers of German rearmament; Britain's overseas role shrank steadily; the European Economic Community never acquired political and military dimensions; serious East–West negotiations were too long delayed and détente collapsed in the late seventies.

Now NATO is no longer an alliance: it is a way of life. Instead of being a means for protecting the independence and survival of Britain, the preservation of NATO has become an end in itself, for which British independence must be sacrificed and British survival risked.

Needless to say, this is not the orthodox view: the opinion of the British defence establishment, of the great majority of the Conservative Party, of moderate members of the Labour Party, of the Social Democratic Party or of many members of the Liberal Party. The received doctrine is that only the threat of American nuclear retaliation deters the Russians from invading Western Europe; that only the presence of American soldiers in Germany makes this threat credible either to Russians or to Europeans; and that only a high level of conventional defence, including British forces stationed in Germany, makes this threat acceptable to the Americans. This orthodox doctrine is particularly well entrenched in the defence establishment and the bureaucracy.

Although the orthodox can always count on support from Moscow, their stance is increasingly challenged by British politicians: mainly on the Left, but also Liberals and a few members of the right wing of the Conservative Party. Their criticisms are echoed by different minorities among the electorate. The predominantly pacifist attitudes of the Campaign for Nuclear Disarmament are reinforced by the supporters, mainly but not exclusively Labour, of non-nuclear defence policies. Opposition to NATO's nuclear strategy has been reinforced by the stationing in England of American cruise missiles under full American control.

Even in right-wing and far from pacifist circles, the deployment of these weapons is seen as compromising British independence and offering to both Super Powers the option of a limited nuclear war from which their own metropolitan territories would be excluded. There is a Gaullist Right in Britain which is no happier than the Left with the proliferation of American military bases (over a hundred) in the British Isles and with the absence of British political control over American military personnel and their weapons. It is not easy to envisage any successor government adopting quite so submissive a policy in this respect as has Mrs Thatcher. Indeed, the annual party conference in October 1986 committed both Labour and Neil Kinnock personally to seeking the removal of all American nuclear weapons from Britain and stricter control over such non-nuclear bases as the United States were permitted to retain in Britain.

Again, for those who believe public opinion polls, 51 per cent of the British were against American missiles in Britain; 56 per cent in favour of the British nuclear deterrent.

Another important aspect of discontent with present British defence policy is the feeling, strongest on the Left but not unknown on the Right, that Britain is doing more than her fair share: keeping forces on the Continent to defend a far richer Germany; spending a higher proportion of her national income on defence; turning herself into an expendable forward base for the United States.

Because the defence tail has for years tended to wag the diplomatic dog in Britain, these military grievances are reflected in the field of foreign affairs. There is, for instance, a view that Britain, indeed Europe, is being needlessly involved in the struggle between the Super Powers for global predominance. This attitude – mainly, but not only, to be found in the Labour Party – needs to be contrasted with the conviction of the Establishment that nothing is more important than the support of the United States. The special relationship with that country has long been very unequal, but it is all that still keeps Britain on a respectable footing among countries that are richer, more efficient, of greater significance in the world.

Many British politicians, by no means all of them Conservative, are prepared to make almost any concession to retain the enhanced national and personal status conferred by American patronage. In a way the British are caught in a vicious circle. Today we are poor because, during the last four decades, we gave too much priority to prestige. But prestige is still more important to Britain than to most European countries, precisely because we are poor.

This is a sharper picture of British divisions on foreign policy and defence than most practising politicians would accept. Their arguments are about points of detail and shades of difference in their treatment. How far should we go in pressing the Community for money; in manifesting disapproval of South Africa; in distancing ourselves from United States policy in Central America; in cultivating better relations with Eastern Europe? Can Britain afford Trident? Ought she to have any nuclear weapons at all? For and against cruise missiles; maritime strategy versus continental commitment; how to cut the defence budget?

In normal circumstances this is about as far as candidates at the next general election are likely to push their questions. If the Conservatives lose, it would be reasonable to expect the cancellation of Trident, defence cuts, less support for hard-line American policies. If the Alliance hold a key position, there might also be a swing towards the Community. Normally, however, one would not regard British withdrawal from the Community or from NATO as serious possibilities. Leaving NATO, admittedly, was suggested at the Labour Party Conference in 1986, but the proposal was heavily defeated.

Even the removal of all nuclear weapons and bases from British soil and waters, which has been a Labour Party commitment since 1983 and was much reiterated in 1986, is still regarded with some scepticism. Previous Labour governments did not always implement in office the nuclear policies they had proclaimed in opposition. Now they may really intend to keep promises which their opponents will not, while campaigning for votes, allow them to forget. As an electoral issue defence offers the Conservatives a welcome distraction from such distressing subjects as unemployment.

It is the conventional wisdom of British politics that defence and foreign policy are not the issues that decide elections. There is even a case for arguing that past changes in these policies have come as a response to economic difficulties at home or new developments abroad rather than as a deliberate implementation of the manifesto of the victorious party. With the decay of consensus in British politics both these arguments seemed less convincing as the eighties neared their end. Nuclear weapons, in particular, do seem to interest many voters and on this issue the Conservative and Labour parties, to a lesser extent the Alliance, offer a choice of sharply different policies. If Labour win a general election and do what they have promised, the removal of nuclear weapons from the British Isles would entail a larger and more sudden change of defence and foreign policy than Britain has known for many years. The potential repercussions are not easy to predict, but it may safely be said that they would be felt at home as well as abroad.

13 The Special Problem of Ulster

Many years ago I listened to a lecture by Dr Garrett Fitzgerald, not then Irish Prime Minister, about the future of Northern Ireland. By the end of the first hour he had just reached the beginning of the nineteenth-century. In this age of ignorance the Irish are among the few peoples who still know their own history.

That history must here be drastically compressed. When the Romans left England, the civilised but not very warlike inhabitants at first managed to resist attack by the wild men of Ireland and Caledonia, but were soon overcome by German and Scandinavian invaders. These were a rough lot, who drove into the Welsh mountains such native English as they did not slaughter or enslave. The bellicose character of the new English nation engendered by these Saxons and Danes was given its cutting edge by the Norman Conquest. Now imbued with a Gallic sense of purpose the English set out to unite the British Isles – a task in which the Romans had failed. It proved to be long and arduous, but it succeeded in both Scotland and Wales because mutual assimilation was possible. England itself was ruled first by a Welsh dynasty (the Tudors), then by a Scottish (the Stuarts). Ireland was only conquered; there was no blending of the peoples.

So, at about the same time as the colonisation of New England, King James I of England and VI of Scotland began the Plantation of Ulster: the settlement in Northern Ireland of emigrants from Scotland. In terms of assimilation it was not a success. Not only were the new arrivals Protestant (that was the object of the exercise) and the Irish Catholic, but these incoming Scots turned out to be Presbyterians – an extreme form of Protestantism that even King James had no desire to encourage. It was as unwelcome to the Irish as the immigrants themselves.

The remedy adopted in North America – elimination of the aboriginal inhabitants – was not available in Ireland, where the native Irish were and remained a majority. In the centuries that followed, therefore, Ireland as a whole was never assimilated to the rest of Great Britain and remained a source of constant trouble and anxiety to governments in London. These favoured the Protestants, on whom alone they could rely, thereby further alienating the Catholics.

By the beginning of this century, Ireland had become such a nuisance that the British Government decided they must get rid of it, whatever the strategic risks – Ireland had been a route favoured by foreign invaders. No British government, however, has ever understood Irish problems and this one under-estimated those Scottish Presbyterians in the North. These had no intention of finding themselves a minority in a Catholic state: a state, what is more, where that Church enjoyed a position of special privilege and influence. As Presbyterians, true descendants of those Covenanters who had shocked even Cromwell by their intolerance, they announced their readiness for armed rebellion. As Scots they were assimilated in a way most of the Irish were not: enjoying much support in the British Conservative Party and the British Army.

They were also – and this is a point not generally understood abroad – a group that was geographically compact, economically dominant, yet spread across the whole range of classes, rooted in the country for centuries, yet conscious of a separate solidarity that transcended the normal social divisions. It was not a colonial situation, in which the ruling class is of exotic origin; spends only a working life in the territory; occupies only a limited range of jobs and is sharply distinguished by upbringing, culture, language and even race from the indigenous inhabitants, the ruled. It was not an Algerian situation, in which the 'colons', however rooted in the country and however diversified their occupations, were so scattered across the entire territory as to be everywhere a small and readily distinguishable minority.

In many of the areas where they had settled these descendants of English and Scottish Presbyterians constituted a large majority of the population. Unfortunately there were no cities and few rural areas where the Catholic minority was insignificant. Without a large transfer of populations it would not have been possible to create an economically viable territory that was homogeneous in terms of religion. The solution actually adopted in the early twenties of this century was to constitute a province of Northern Ireland with a population two-thirds Protestant and one-third Catholic, which would remain an integral part of the United Kingdom of Great Britain and Northern Ireland, while the rest of Ireland, with four-fifths of the area and two-thirds of the population of the whole island, would become first self-governing and then wholly independent.

Northern Ireland was also largely autonomous, with its own

parliament and government at Stormont. Defence, foreign affairs and other central policies were reserved to the parliament at Westminster, to which Northern Ireland also elected members. This partition aroused much opposition among Irish Catholics, but was accepted in Great Britain and, even in Ireland, commanded a grudging acquiescence as preferable to the civil war that had already caused much suffering, particularly in Southern Ireland.

On neither side of the border, however, did Irish politics take a normal course after independence. Instead of dividing between Left and Right, Southern politicians were grouped in terms of the methods they advocated for ending partition (an objective enshrined in the Southern constitution). In the North the split was between Protestant Loyalists and Catholics aspiring to absorption by the South. Although there were links between the (Protestant) Unionist Party in Northern Ireland and the Conservatives in Great Britain, such Socialists as emerged in Ulster lacked the strength or the faith to establish ideological ties or to assert common economic, social or class interests across the border or even across the Irish Channel. With every decade that passed, it became harder for the English, Scots and Welsh to understand what increasingly seemed to them the archaic character of Irish politics.

In the North the Protestants used their two-thirds majority to entrench their own dominance of the state and to discriminate against the minority: not, so they claimed, because the minority were Catholics, but because they were disloyal. A blind eye was turned to these practices in London as long as they succeeded in keeping Northern Ireland relatively quiet at a time when the strategic importance of the province was growing: with the loss of British bases in Southern Ireland; with Dublin tilting to neutrality; and with the obvious approach of war with Germany. When war did come, however, it was thought prudent to exempt Northern Ireland from compulsory military service.

From the beginning of the twenties until the end of the sixties Northern Ireland was ruled, in most matters of daily concern to the inhabitants, by the Protestant majority of the Northern Irish themselves. The London government might extend to Northern Ireland the benefits of post-war reforms – the 1948 National Health Service Act, for instance, but it was Stormont who implemented such measures. A couple of British regiments had their peace-time stations in Ulster, but were seldom needed to assist in quelling disturbances.

Law and order, internal security and justice were the responsibility of Stormont, who maintained, by British standards, unusually large and well-armed police forces for this purpose.

Northern Ireland was not a colony. Constitutionally, politically and socially it was, in those years, more like one of the southern states of the United States: Alabama, say, though the Catholics of Northern Ireland were never as badly off as black Americans.

In the sixties, however, Northern Ireland began to feel, as did Southern America, the impact of the civil rights movement. There being no segregation or apartheid in Ulster, Catholic demands tended to focus on such issues as more equitable representation on public bodies and among government employees or a fairer share of public expenditure on housing or schools. Official efforts to introduce a single educational system had, however, been defeated by the opposition of both communities.

With the post-war expansion of the Welfare State there was now more interest and sympathy for such issues in Great Britain as well as a greater power of the purse. Even Terence O'Neill, who became Prime Minister of Northern Ireland in 1963, wanted to make some concession to Catholic aspirations.

In this he was ahead of his Protestant supporters, whose persistent opposition finally drove him from office in 1969. Meanwhile events had followed the classic pattern: each minor concession to the Catholics prompted usually well justified demands for more; successes and setbacks alike tended to broaden the movement and to shift the tactics from petitions to processions; the more publicly visible the Catholic protesters became, the sharper was the Protestant backlash; as conflict grew rougher, so the real revolutionaries began to take over the leadership from the respectable, middle-class liberals who had begun it all. This unfortunate process led to a number of violent incidents in 1968 and early 1969, culminating in major sectarian riots in both Belfast and Londonderry in mid-August 1969.

Because the Northern Irish Police (known as the Royal Ulster Constabulary – RUC) lost control and behaved with anti-Catholic bias, the British Government were forced into a decision they had tried hard – too hard – to avoid: to deploy units of the British regular army.

Ministers had been right to shrink from this desperate step, but wrong to be half-hearted when they finally took it. If the Army have to intervene at all in civil disturbances, it should be in overwhelming strength, with a clear political mandate and the authority to use such force as may be necessary. That did not happen in August 1969.

It was generally recognised that the Army had come to provide Northern Catholics with the protection against Protestant mob violence (burning down whole streets in Belfast, for instance) that had not been forthcoming from the predominantly Protestant police force at the disposal of the Northern Ireland Government. But there were not enough British soldiers (initially only three battalions) to cow the Protestants, reassure the Catholics and stop dead the rioting. Violence was reduced, but both sides continued to resort to what they called self-defence. The Army, being under the usual orders to use minimum force, spent much time standing between the contestants under a hail of missiles from the youth of both religions.

Being accustomed to foreign soldiers who employed rougher tactics – in Hungary or the Lebanon – it was with astonishment that I watched their ordeal on television: itself as potent an influence in this conflict as in others of the second half of the twentieth-century. Of course, it was not long before, in self-defence, even the British Army adopted a less passive stance and relations with the civilian population worsened.

This was particularly true of the Catholics. The Army had come to save them, but, arriving too late and in numbers that were inadequate for full success, received no lasting gratitude. Their subsequent display of patience under provocation had forfeited the awe of both communities. And, among the Catholics, there were elements anxious to make the worst of both weaknesses.

Hindsight is easy and usually misleading, but it does seem conceivable that four times as many soldiers, arriving a week earlier and firing on any rioters disobeying orders to disperse, might have spared Ulster fifteen years of death and destruction.

As it was, British compromise had the usual effect of alienating both communities. Protestant grievances were inevitable: the London government insisted on curtailing the ability of Stormont to use the police against the Catholics, but did not themselves succeed in imposing law and order. This was in part because Catholics, having seen too few British soldiers arrive too late to save them, now preferred themselves to erect barricades and to take other measures for the local defence of the districts they inhabited. In this display of alienation, so provocative to the Protestants and so subversive of any kind of government, the Catholics were deliberately and successfully encouraged by the Irish Republican Army, the IRA.

The IRA, if I may drastically simplify its history, began in 1916 with the mission of expelling the British from Ireland and establishing by force an united and independent republic throughout the entire island.

The IRA relied, as did the Palestine Liberation Organisation and for the same reasons, on guerrilla warfare and terrorism. Until the Treaty of 1922 establishing two states in Ireland, the IRA did operate against the British Army and its British auxiliaries, the notorious Black and Tans, though even then most of its victims were Irish.

After 1922 the IRA operated almost exclusively against Irishmen: those in the South who had betrayed Ireland by preferring four-fifths of a loaf to no bread, the government, parliament and supporters of the 26-county Irish Free State; and those Northern, but still Irish, upholders of Protestant autonomy. Only rarely were the British themselves attacked, on the few occasions when British soldiers stationed in Northern Ireland had to help local security forces, or in the two campaigns of the IRA in Great Britain itself.

The first of these, in 1938–9, involved bombs in post-boxes, bicycles and left-luggage offices, inflicted some random civilian casualties, attracted German and American support, but had little political impact. The second, in the early fifties, was intended to acquire weapons and, thanks to disgraceful weaknesses in British Army security, had some success. The campaign for which these weapons were needed was in Northern Ireland and failed, largely because the IRA had by now succeeded in frightening the Dublin government (which they did not, of course, recognise) as much as that in Belfast. By about 1962, therefore, tacit cooperation across the border had virtually defeated the IRA. In the words of a notably sympathetic historian of the IRA, it 'was a husk – its strength eroded, its purpose lost, its future unclear'.

As the old rhyme has it:

'When the Devil was sick, the Devil a monk would be
When the Devil was well, the Devil a monk would he.'

The IRA turned to political action and proclaimed as their objective 'a 32-County Workers' and Small Farmers' Republic'. There had, of course, always been a strand of socialism in the traditions of the IRA and in 1932 the Catholic and Protestant workers of Belfast had badly frightened Stormont by joining forces to demand higher unemployment relief – which they got.

On the face of it, striving for proletarian solidarity across the border seemed a more promising, if more gradual, approach to Irish unity than trying to bomb the North into submission. It was not, however, an approach which appealed to the financial backers of the IRA in the

The Special Problem of Ulster 135

South or in the United States or to many in the IRA itself. To them a socialist was a Marxist and a Marxist was an atheist and an atheist was almost as bad as a Protestant. The success of the IRA in encouraging and infiltrating the Civil Rights movement of the sixties seemed a dubious achievement to these old-style militants and their paymasters. When it also turned out that the leadership had been caught unawares by the rioting of August 1969, indignation reinforced ideological disagreement and, with some help from a Dublin government anxious for a quiet life in the South, the IRA split into the Officials and the Provisionals.

It is the latter, commonly known as the Provos, who have incited, organised and carried out most of the subsequent terrorism in Northern Ireland and, to a lesser extent, in Southern Ireland and Great Britain itself. The violence of Protestant para-military groups was on a smaller scale and more sectarian than revolutionary in character. During those sixteen years a variety of expedients have been attempted by all sides. The IRA have alternated between application of the now classic formula – indiscriminate terror will provoke repression which will alienate the population from the authorities – and terrorism more selectively directed against British rather than Irish targets. The latter is intended to disgust the people of Great Britain with the very idea of continued responsibility for Northern Ireland.

The British governments of the seventies and eighties tried not only to repress terrorism, but to seek some political compromise capable of commanding the acquiescence of both Catholics and Protestants. In pursuit of the first objective they tried interning suspected terrorists, only to abandon the expedient as being more provocative than effective. At one stage they greatly reinforced the Army to take over security duties from a police force unacceptable to the Catholics. Later they reduced the size and role of the Army in favour of a reformed police. The operations of soldiers and policemen, no less than those of the IRA, have become steadily more sophisticated, but not always more successful.

On the political front the endeavour has consistently been to reconcile the Catholic minority to the existence of Northern Ireland without thereby driving the Protestant majority into open revolt. One of the first steps was the suspension, in 1972, of the autonomous, but always Protestant-dominated government and parliament of Northern Ireland. The next 14 years were devoted to vain attempts to devise improved models to replace these institutions and escape from what had been intended as the transitional burden of direct rule from London.

One high point was the so-called Sunningdale Agreement of 1973 by which Catholic and Protestant politicians in Northern Ireland were persuaded to accept arrangements for power-sharing in a new Northern Ireland Executive. This body would itself be represented, together with the Dublin government, on a Council of Ireland with rather vaguely defined responsibility for the common concerns of Belfast and Dublin.

Before this agreement could be properly implemented, it had split the Unionist Party in Northern Ireland and led to a strike backed by both Protestant trade unions and paramilitary organisations. The former controlled the power stations and the latter intimidated those who might have wanted to work. In London, meanwhile, the Conservative Government that negotiated the Sunningdale Agreement had been replaced by a Labour Government reluctant to break a strike by using the Army, themselves doubtful of their ability to take over the entire task of electricity generation.

So the British Government and their successors fell back on direct rule.

In November 1985 a renewed British attempt at compromise, involving a kind of observer status for the Dublin government, again aroused Protestant hostility. Ulster Unionist Members of Parliament in London resigned their seats in a House of Commons where a large majority of members of other parties had endorsed the Anglo-Irish agreement signed at Hillsborough. In January 1986 the Unionists won 14 out of 15 by-elections in Northern Ireland, but only 44 per cent of the electorate supported them. In March Protestant resentment was further emphasised by a 24-hour strike and, in April, by what seemed to the mainland British the suicidal strategy of a terrorist campaign against the reformed, but still predominantly Protestant, Royal Ulster Constabulary. That, at least, was not long sustained.

The raw winter of 1985–6 thus cast a chill on British hopes that the gradual improvement of security in Ulster and of cooperation from Dublin might engender some readiness for compromise. Nothing was expected from the IRA, whose persistent violence in Ulster was matched by occasional outrages in England: the bombing of shoppers at Harrods in 1983 or of the Conservative Party Conference in 1984. But over a decade and a half of British military support and financial subsidy seemed to have earned neither trust nor gratitude from Protestants professing to be 'unionists' and 'loyalists'. In February

The Special Problem of Ulster 137

1986 the Conservative Prime Minister of the United Kingdom warned Ulster Unionists (her words echoed by a leading member of the Labour Party) of the danger that their conduct might erode mainland support for the continued inclusion of Ulster in the United Kingdom.

The main burden, of course, has fallen on the people of Northern Ireland, but even this must be kept in proportion. In 1980 terrorism caused 76 deaths: motor accidents 289. The ratio of terrorist deaths to population matched homicides in Luxembourg, but was only one-tenth of the score in Detroit. Ordinary crime, incidentally, is less prevalent in Northern Ireland than in England and Wales. In 1984 there were 64 terrorist deaths in Northern Ireland, including 9 British soldiers and 12 of the IRA. The total fell in 1985, but more policemen suffered.

Although some reinforcements had to be sent in 1986, the number of British troops deployed in Northern Ireland has steadily declined. But the net cost to English, Scottish and Welsh taxpayers of such consequences of unrest as higher unemployment is now in the region of a billion pounds a year.

The IRA have undoubtedly made Ulster a dead loss to the mainland British. They have also successfully bombed those million Protestants in Northern Ireland into hating Irish unity, Catholics and compromise more than ever before. They have persuaded the governing class in the South to fear the prospect of absorbing Northern Catholics and to shrink from the nightmare of integrating Northern Protestants. Agreement is less likely today than it has ever been.

Genocide is not feasible for the IRA, which is numerically rather small. The notion – cherished by some of their members and foreign supporters – that enough terror would eventually persuade the British to use their own army to disarm Ulster Protestants and force them into an united Ireland is insane. All that is left is the idea that the Ulster Protestants are an imaginary bogey created by the British, so they will meekly submit themselves to the IRA, to Dublin and to Rome, as soon as the last British soldier withdraws.

No one in his senses believes that. What many in England, Scotland and Wales, by now disgusted with everything Irish, do rather wistfully hope is that the announcement of a date for total withdrawal would wonderfully concentrate Irish minds and, after some fighting not involving us, lead to compromise. The worst that could happen, these people argue, is that the Northern Protestants would try to teach the Catholics a lesson; that Dublin would intervene; and that the ensuing civil war would be fought by the Irish and on Irish soil.

Not all the precedents are encouraging. We set a date for pulling out of India in 1947, come what might. What came included half a million dead and a couple of wars already. The consequences of a similar decision in 1948 in Palestine are familiar and are not yet over. But, India and Palestine being reasonably distant, at least no more British soldiers have been killed in those countries and Britain herself has arguably lost much less by withdrawing than it would have cost to stay.

Ireland, unfortunately, is only thirty miles away.

Nor is that the worst of it. The 1981 census found that 850 000 inhabitants of England, Scotland and Wales had been born in Ireland. American experience suggests that those of Irish descent often retain an Irish loyalty for more than one generation. Counting those born in Britain and thus not identified, as many as 1.5 million in mainland Britain, about the population of Northern Ireland, may have some cause to feel themselves Irish. Glasgow, Liverpool, Manchester and London are known to contain substantial numbers.

This is something to be remembered by those English, Scots and Welsh understandably inclined to take water and wash their hands of the problems of Ireland. To those problems no solution has yet been suggested likely to command widespread approval, even acquiescence. The consequences of mere disengagement might be felt on both sides of the Irish Channel.

14 Civil Liberties in Britain

'Civil liberties' is a more convenient title than 'civil rights', for that term has acquired in the United States the narrower meaning of 'rights of ethnic minorities'. 'Human rights' would be a misleading alternative, for different nations – even the same nations in different eras – have had very various ideas about the 'rights' or the 'liberties' their citizens are entitled to expect.

In the British Isles, for instance, one of the questions disputed for centuries was religious toleration. Which doctrines might be freely professed and which should be persecuted? Today no sect, not even non-Christian religions, has anything to fear in Britain (Ulster always excepted) but ignorance and apathy. Tolerance does not extend to breaches of the civil law (extortion or child-marriage, for instance), but it is in Moslem and Communist countries that deviations from orthodoxy are punished by the State nowadays.

Any society must, of course, impose some restrictions on the conduct of its members or they could not go on living together, least of all in the crowded conditions of the British Isles. If liberty were defined as the right of the individual to do as he pleases, then that individual could scarcely avoid falling a victim to the displeasing desires of others. Leaving aside what is generally reckoned as ordinary crime, the balance between social constraint and personal choice is the measure of civil liberty, but it is no absolute standard, nor is it at all easy to define. Liberty and licence; order and oppression are two sides of the same coins. The most that can be attempted here is to identify some of the features that distinguish the present balance in Britain from that of other periods or different countries.

Naturally civil liberties are as much a subject of controversy as any other political issue. The Liberals have the broadest notion of the bounds of individual freedom. The Conservative regard for private enterprise is balanced by their concern for the political power of the State. This is no less important, though for different reasons, to the Left, who must also have regard to the corporate interests of the trade unions and the working class. All parties accord liberty most priority when in opposition. Perhaps there is a wider tendency, on issues not already involving rivalry among the political parties, to regard the absence of regulations as a positive gain for liberty.

The citizens of many otherwise liberty-loving European countries accept the duty to tell the police who lives in their house, to carry an identity card and to do military service. The British suffered similar infractions of their liberty during the Second World War and for some years thereafter, but no longer. In 1950, for instance, the Lord Chief Justice, whose enthusiasm for hanging and flogging excited the horror of liberally minded Englishmen, denounced the retention of identity cards with such indignation that he shamed the British Government of the day into abolishing them.

This was all the more remarkable because the twentieth-century has seen many more serious infringements of civil liberties in Britain. In 1974, for instance, the Prevention of Terrorism Act gave the police greatly increased powers to arrest suspects, to detain them for questioning and to search their homes. In anything that falls under that large, vague umbrella – Security – the rights of Britons, from Habeas Corpus onwards, have been much eroded, but with much less general complaint than over identity cards.

But there are also very different conceptions in Britain of what constitutes civil liberties. One of the reasons, of course, is that we have no written constitution, no positive law listing the rights of the citizen. Although we have ratified the European Convention on Human Rights, we have not embodied it in our domestic law. Those who wish to profit by some of its provisions must take their grievance to a foreign court. The whole question of civil liberties in Britain is tangled up in a cat's cradle of statutes and precedents, not written down in a book that anyone can consult in a public library. So many people think we need a Bill of Rights, which the House of Lords passed in 1986 and sent for consideration by the House of Commons under the title of The Human Rights and Fundamental Freedoms Bill.

What makes this such a controversial idea – apart from the probable loss of business by lawyers – is that there are at least three different categories of rights: the rights of individuals; the collective rights of organisations or combinations; and the rights of the State or, if you prefer an optimistic view, of the community. These three kinds of right frequently conflict and their development has followed different paths.

In most countries of the world the rights of the individual, certainly those of the educated, male, reasonably prosperous individual, have declined over the last century or so. In Victorian times, for instance, anyone could walk into a chemist's shop and buy any drug, medicine, poison or other chemical he cared to ask for. Laudanum, a preparation of opium, was widely consumed by all classes. Working women used to dose their children when leaving home in the morning to keep them quiet. Nowadays, throughout most of the world, the number of preparations only obtainable on a doctor's prescription is for ever increasing. Ecuador, in 1961, was one of the last countries free from this medical tyranny.

At the beginning of this century, a British traveller did not need even a passport to visit any country in the world except Russia and Turkey. Today, to go anywhere outside Western Europe, he must have a great deal more. In practice, rather than in strict law, a passport is again needed, as in the time of Queen Elizabeth I, to get out of the country. Among countries reputed free, perhaps only the United States are more restrictive.

It is, of course, to serve the State, or even the community, that these and other fetters are imposed on the individual. Customs vary. In Bonn, for instance, householders may not mow their lawn on a Sunday; in parts of the United States citizens may freely purchase machine-guns; Moslem countries try ever harder to eradicate those profane and sensual pleasures which support an ever growing share of the industry and commerce of Christian nations. Even within Britain itself there are curious inconsistencies. In April 1986 the Thatcher Government tried to introduce a bill allowing shops to open on Sundays, but were defeated in the House of Commons by the combined supporters of religion and of shop assistants. Was this a victory or a defeat for the cause of civil liberty?

Perhaps the most important test of civil liberties, in Britain as in other countries, springs from that question of Lenin's I quoted earlier: Who? Whom? Who is free to do what?

In law, for instance, the police cannot compel anyone to go to a police station unless they arrest him. If questioned he need not answer, must be told of this right if charged or even suspected. He must be brought before a magistrate within 24 hours, has the right to see a solicitor, cannot be photographed or fingerprinted without his consent or the authority of a magistrate and, if denied his rights, can apply to the courts for a writ of Habeas Corpus to regain his liberty. These rights can legally be restricted in the case of those arrested under the politically controversial Prevention of Terrorism Act. Even those arrested on other grounds sometimes find such rights difficult to exercise if they happen to be young, poor, uneducated, black, Irish or otherwise suspect.

Because more crime, particularly political crime, is nowadays committed by members of the middle class than was the case in earlier times, it has become obvious that those suspected by the police are not invariably accorded their full legal rights. Nor can they always expect redress from the courts. Evidence improperly obtained is often admitted and only 8 per cent of applications for Habeas Corpus are successful. I do not suggest that we have become a Police State or that the police are usually oppressive or brutal, but respectable citizens are more at risk than they used to be – in part because there are fewer respectable citizens than there used to be.

I do not know whether an Englishman's house ever really was his castle, but it is certainly not so today. The number of tax, customs, public health, gas, water, electricity and telephone officials authorised to enter, sometimes with notice, sometimes without, usually armed with a magistrate's warrant, but not always, is alarming. Nor do British judges look with the same charity as their American and European counterparts on the householder who defends his home with firearms.

Although the police normally need a warrant to enter and search premises, they may do so if it becomes urgently necessary to make an arrest. Given the prevalence today of armed terrorists and violent criminals, it is scarcely surprising to read, once or twice a month, that the police have broken down a door and burst into a house at four in the morning. Occasionally one of the inmates is accidentally shot in the process. In our unhappy era, less drastic methods would allow terrorists to perpetrate more atrocities or expose the police to unjustifiable risks. In my youth, however, it was supposed that such dramas occurred only in Nazi Germany or the Soviet Union.

When the British subject leaves his home and forsakes the even tenor of his personal or his working existence for the stormy seas of politics, he has always been at risk. He has never had any positive right to meet and demonstrate in public places, let alone highways, which he is expected to traverse from a reputable starting-point to a respectable destination – and, of course, back again. In practice meetings, demonstrations and processions are seldom prohibited or prevented, but permission is sometimes required and it is usually prudent to consult the police. If authority is ill-disposed, almost any conduct can be construed as the offence of obstructing the highway or provoking a breach of the peace. Authority is usually tolerant until demonstrations lead to actual riot and most complaints concern the understandable efforts of the police to prevent known enemies from confronting one another: Communists and Fascists, for instance.

As in other aspects of the civil liberties of the individual, administrative practice can be more important than legal principles.

British practice is not noticeably less liberal than that of most comparable nations. In strict law, however, the citizen has few positive rights and authority is on the whole less indulgent than it used to be.

There is one important exception. Liberty to write, publish and broadcast all manner of opinions is greater today than ever before. Prosecutions for sedition, blasphemy, obscenity and the like have become rare and even less often successful. The State, the constitution and conventional morality may be attacked with impunity by writers – provided they avoid personal defamation – even in cases where speeches to crowds or the organisation of processions and demonstrations might attract legal sanctions.

It can still be argued, by those willing to take a broad view of the question, that the civil liberties of the individual Briton are in many respects rather above the average enjoyed by citizens of the industrialised democracies. If, during the twentieth century, the State has encroached, this has been mainly on the rights of male members of the middle and upper classes. Women, children, the destitute and handicapped, deviants and, all things considered, members of the working class are better off than they were. Many individuals, even whole categories of individual, still have legitimate grievances. But, in recent decades, much of the debate in Britain has been less concerned with the rights and liberties of individuals, as individuals, than with their collective privileges.

This has had some curious results. The National Council for Civil Liberties – an independent organisation – recently split because some of its members could not agree that the right *not* to strike was just as important as the right to strike.

For most of this century it has been accepted in most countries, including Britain, that citizens should have the right to combine, in trade unions, in political parties, in all kinds of associations, in order to obtain collectively what they would be unable to obtain individually. In most countries, again including Britain, the State has also sought, not always successfully, to restrain some citizens from combining and to limit the methods of persuasion they may employ. In Britain, but not in all European countries, neither the police nor the armed forces have the right to go on strike.

Not all classes of citizen have the same rights, though the general trend is towards uniformity. Legally, women are still not on quite the same footing as men, but almost everybody now agrees that women should have the right to vote, to become Members of Parliament, even to rise to the position of Prime Minister. I say 'almost', because some people have serious reservations about the last proposition.

It can nevertheless be argued (though some male historians disagree) that the women of Britain, the present Prime Minister included, owe their political rights to a violent campaign of organised disaffection in the early years of the twentieth century. The use of similar means for political ends today would certainly excite the disapproval of Margaret Thatcher.

That was one of the more dramatic episodes in the long retreat conducted by the British governing class, the judges always fighting valiantly in the rearguard, from the original position that politics was the business of Parliament and that participation by the ordinary (meaning prosperous, male) citizen should be confined to participation in the election of members of parliament. Until quite recently this retreat was generally regarded as progress, the argument being that many legitimate grievances would never have been remedied if aggrieved citizens had not joined forces to make themselves a nuisance.

Within the last twenty years, however, there has been some reaction against this view, in Britain as in other countries. Many of those who made themselves a nuisance seemed actually to have rejected the ordinary political process as too biased or too slow. The grievances for which they sought redress were not always their own or obviously within the competence of the British state. Students, for instance, became prominent among the rivals of the State because of the wrongs suffered by such foreigners as were in fashion: Chileans, Greeks, South African negroes, Vietnamese. The victims of their troublemaking were not the foreign governments responsible and even the British government were put to less inconvenience than ordinary members of the public.

The latter, rather than employers, also became the principal victims of strikes. Trade unions sometimes seemed, even to their own members, as powerful and as oppressive as big corporations. Public manifestations of protest, hitherto the expedient of those to whom society had given unequal treatment and denied an equal voice, were now employed by minorities seeking to impose their will on others. The right of the individual not to strike began to receive some of the popular consideration previously concentrated on the freedom of action of the union.

Persons professing unpopular opinions began to realise – when they wished to express their views in a newspaper or a public speech – that the obstacles were no longer the same as in earlier periods of British history. They now had much less to fear from the servants than from the rivals of the State. In 1986 actors and actresses – once considered so free as necessarily to be libertine – were forbidden on pain of professional disqualification to perform in South Africa. No peacetime British government for much more than a century would have ventured to impose such a ban, which was decided by a politically active minority in the strangely-named trade union EQUITY.

One result of the trends of recent decades has been that the liberty-loving Briton now has more enemies than the State. In the past the right of citizens to combine their forces to promote reform has brought the people much advantage. It remains easy to list other changes that might be desirable, but I believe there is more freedom of most kinds in Britain today than there was when I was a boy. It is no longer obvious, however, that future progress will always result in increased liberty. Nor can the majority necessarily expect greater freedom to flow from redressing even the genuine grievances of minorities.

Among these aggrieved minorities must be reckoned the coloured communities. There is unfortunately no doubt at all that racial prejudice and racial discrimination are rampant in Britain. Few people can claim to be entirely guiltless in this respect, but much of the blame must go to the politicians and officials responsible not merely for allowing, but for encouraging the massive immigration of the decade and a half that followed the Second World War. Employers greedy for cheap labour and Commonwealth sentimentalists may have known no better, but there were then in positions of power and influence men with the personal experience, or the education, to realise that the British remained what they had always been: notorious among the nations for their chauvinism.

In our history immigrants have always been unpopular. In the eighteenth century the Scots were detested in England as, during the nineteenth, were the Irish in Scotland. Because my grandfather left Scotland, I am regarded in that country as a 'furriner'. Buying a country cottage in Wales is not without its risks for the English today. As for French Huguenots, Flemish weavers, Jews, Poles and many others, they had various claims on British hospitality, they all brought Britain many benefits, but they suffered in their early years in this country.

Not since the Norman Conquest, however, had there been an influx so large and so visibly different. In 1945 there were experienced trade union leaders among our ministers. They must have known what the reactions of their members would be. For many years before the Second World War successive British governments had been forced to operate tight immigration controls because of the understandable fears of British trade unions that every alien admitted meant one less job for British workers at a time of massive unemployment.

That particular fear was less relevant in the full employment of the forties and fifties, but the shortage of houses, of decent houses, above all, of cheap houses was well known. Even those optimists who thought there would always be enough jobs for the new arrivals might have wondered where they were going to live.

Because British politicians took no thought for the morrow, there developed ghettoes: over-crowded, insanitary, condemning the immigrants to an inferior existence, reinforcing the prejudice of the natives that it was the immigrants themselves who were inferior. Even that might gradually have been overcome if the post-war boom had continued at its original pace or if the volume of immigration had declined with the demand for their labour. Neither happened. Long before the whole bubble burst, the immigrants in quest of unskilled jobs and cheap accommodation had begun grossly to exceed the supply.

The reaction of successive governments of both parties was to restrict the continuing flow of immigrants. This was too late, was not accompanied by effective measures to provide jobs and houses for those who had already arrived and served to encourage the ever more intense feeling among the natives that immigration was the cause of all the problems and difficulties experienced by the poorer classes. The legislation passed with laudable intention of combating racial prejudice and discrimination often did more to irritate the natives than to relieve the immigrants. Moreover, the subordinate servants of the State – police, immigration officers, the officials of the social security services – tended to share the prejudices of the populace.

The understandable reaction of the coloured communities, whether immigrant or, as time passed, increasingly native-born, was to huddle together for mutual protection. They also strove to preserve their distinctive languages, culture and way of life. They shrank from inter-marriage – not that most of them would have found this easy. They cannot be blamed, but assimilation would have facilitated acceptance.

The treatment of the coloured minority in Britain is the blackest stain on any British claim to a respectable record for civil liberties or the maintenance of a tolerant and civilised society. The racist prejudice of the natives was foreseeable. Britain's rulers should either have accepted it as inevitable and excluded all coloured immigrants or, if they were resolved to defy popular sentiment, should have paid the necessary price in terms of new laws, additional public expenditure and positive discrimination. They did neither, but just let it all happen.

As a result the coloured citizens of Britain do not today receive equal treatment or equal liberty – not in law, but in practice. It is not an adequate excuse that other civilised nations also have minorities with similar causes of complaint.

If we leave aside the poor and the handicapped, whose grievances are of quite a different kind, immigrants are the principal victims of the present social and political system in Britain. They are in a different category from those citizens who, in pursuit of gain or from motives of a political character, deliberately defy the law in order to vex their fellows.

In February 1970, for instance, the Garden House Hotel in Cambridge thought they would earn a little extra money by organising a Greek evening: Greek food, Greek wine and Greek music. When the guests arrived they were greeted by some 400 demonstrators, many of them undergraduates of the university, who broke windows, overturned tables in the dining-room, frightened a lot of people and, when the police arrive, fought them.

They were not protesting against high prices or bad food and service. Their complaint was that a Greek evening in Cambridge constituted a provocative encouragement to an unpopular government in Athens. Now some of the diners, nostalgic tourists apart, may have had political motives: no sensible gourmet or music-lover would choose a *Greek* evening. But British subjects are entitled to eat even a political dinner in peace and quiet and, although some left-wing writers regarded the prosecution of the leading demonstrators as an infraction of civil liberties, many a peaceable citizen probably approved of the prison sentences imposed.

Violence is often regarded nowadays as a necessary instrument of political change. This is not a view, still less a practice, which has been at all conducive, in recent decades, to the continued growth of civil liberties in Britain. It has, however, required the freedom-loving Briton to be on his guard, as much against the rivals as the servants of the State.

15 The Scope for Change

A week, as Lord Wilson was fond of remarking, is a long time in politics. Sensible writers avoid the kind of forecast that is liable to be out of date before it is printed. In that respect politics differs from meteorology. In Britain long range weather forecasting has been abandoned as inherently unreliable. Projecting a political trend into the next decade, however, can sometimes prove a better bet than guessing what will happen next month. When events assume a pattern, they can also acquire a continuing momentum. What is so difficult is to distinguish the lasting currents of change beneath the surface turbulence.

Alexis de Tocqueville, a French writer, made a famous prediction in 1835. 'Today,' he wrote, 'there are in the world two great peoples who, from different starting-points, seem to be advancing towards the same goal: the Russians and the Americans . . . each of them seems destined by the secret intentions of Providence to hold in his hands the fate of half the world.'

His words are famous because, more than a century afterwards, they ceased to be fantasy and became plausible. Most political prophets are more likely to share the fate of William Pitt, a British Prime Minister of some renown. In 1792 he forecast fifteen years of peace, but war began in 1793 and he had been dead nine years before it ended in 1815.

Such predictions have been out of fashion with British Prime Minister since Neville Chamberlain promised 'peace for our time' on 1 October 1938. His successors have realised they no longer have a free choice, even to the extent enjoyed by Gladstone a century ago, between peace and war. That is only one of the ways in which we are now living in a different historical era.

From the end of the seventeenth century until the early years of the twentieth the British experience was one of progress. Over the years and by comparison with other states Britain's economic and naval strength increased. First in England, then throughout the British Isles, the impact of war was no longer felt on native soil. With occasional setbacks Britain's empire expanded. Her institutions were admired and imitated abroad. Even her rivals admitted the growth of her political influence.

Britain, of course, was never a Super Power: she surpassed others in many respects, but not in all. The security then conferred by her insular status, for instance, allowed her to maintain a much smaller army than other Great Powers. Not all foreigners admitted that Britain was first among equals, but, by the middle of the nineteenth century, that was reckoned in Britain as a modest claim: economically, politically, imperially, however you cared to measure it.

The benefits of this progress were unevenly distributed among the British people. The rich and powerful always received a disproportionate share. Although the poor in Britain were often less wretched than they were abroad, change did, at certain periods, bring actual disadvantage to some classes. The enclosure of common ground helped landowners and improved agriculture, but hurt many of the rural poor. The industrial revolution brought fresh wealth and strength to Britain, but involved the cruel exploitation of a new proletariat. And for the Highland Clearances there was no excuse. All through the nineteenth century emigration was a desperate expedient to which many in Britain, as elsewhere in Europe, had to resort.

Nevertheless, by 1910 the mass of the British people were much better off – by every economic, political or social test – than they had been in 1690. During the years between, the governing class had steadily broadened its political base. Those who thought about such things believed Britain had made great progress, had in most respects made more progress than other countries and would continue to advance in the future. At all times during this period some of the politically aware had been discontented with the then state of the country, but they had usually looked forward with hope and even confidence to the prospect of change.

It was in the second half of the nineteenth century that a few knowledgeable Britons began to fear that future changes might be for the worse. They were particularly concerned by the outlook for the British economy. Through a series of historical accidents Britain had achieved an economic strength out of all proportion to the size of her population or the extent of her natural resources. As late as 1871 Britain had nearly 32 per cent of the world's manufacturing capacity and produced more pig iron, for instance, than the rest of the world put together. It was probably inevitable that more populous nations with better access to raw materials would overtake her in such basic statistics as the output of steel. It was nevertheless unfortunate that Britain did not emulate her rivals, or even such small countries as Sweden or Switzerland, by developing a high technology industry more dependent on skill and education than on raw materials or mass labour.

Although Britain's economic failings were exposed by the First World War, the roots of her decline lie further back. During the twentieth century the process has only occasionally been interrupted and, in the last thirty years, it has actually accelerated. As earlier mentioned, national decline was long politically obscured because the majority of the British people, even if they had fallen behind their foreign counterparts, were better off than their own parents and grandparents. Real personal disposable income per head in Britain almost doubled between 1951 and 1978. Does it matter that other countries did even better?

If it does, this is not because of anything so simple as a loss of national prestige. The significance of ranking sixth or seventh in gross national product or (the published statistics differ considerably from one compilation to another) somewhere between no. 24 and no. 36 in national income per head is that these are milestones on a downhill road. In some ways – unemployment, for instance, or the National Health Service – decline compared to other countries has already meant absolute decline in Britain itself. If the trend continues, deterioration will spread.

In guessing what might happen two points are worth considering. The trend has long been evident and the symptoms of relative decline were usually apparent many years before decline became absolute. Germany overtook Britain as a producer of steel in 1893 and of pig iron in 1906. Measured on its own British output of iron nevertheless went on rising until 1913 and of steel until 1970.

Germany makes a good yardstick by which to judge British performance. In area, population and natural resources Germany was always ahead, but not, as with China, the Soviet Union or the United States, by an order of magnitude. Unlike Japan, another successful rival, Germany's culture, history, political and social structure were broadly similar to Britain's. Germany's wealth did not stem, as did that of Sweden or Switzerland, from a twentieth century passed in peaceful neutrality. On the contrary, the only periods in this century when Britain surpassed Germany economically were those that followed Germany's shattering defeat in two world wars.

If Germany early overtook British production of iron and steel; if she was the first, even in the last century, to develop the newer electrical, chemical, automotive and optical industries; if the gross national product of West Germany alone was more than twice Britain's in 1976; then some explanation is needed of a track record going back a hundred years and lacking any of the obvious historical or geographical excuses that might be invoked when considering some of Britain's other successful rivals. In 1871, let us remember, British national income per head was almost twice Germany's. The flourishing trade between the two countries then comprised an exchange of British manufactures for German agricultural produce. Answers have never been lacking to the question: what went wrong with Britain? As early as 1870, for instance, Lyon Playfair, that far-sighted Scottish professor, had warned 'this country is losing her position among manufacturing nations' by neglecting education, particularly scientific and technical education. That neglect still continues. Britain ranks no. 28 among the nations in what she spends on the schooling of each child. Shortage of money is not the only cause, nor does blame belong to the government alone. The May 1986 report by HM Inspectors of Schools was harsh.

Few involved in providing, or providing for, education can take much – if any – pride in a national service within which three tenths of all the lessons seen were unsatisfactory, one fifth were adversely affected by poor accommodation and a quarter were suffering from shortages of equipment. . . . Taking all institutions together, the most frequently noted factor affecting the work was again the quality of the teaching.

The rivals whose schools have overtaken Britain's also send far more of their children on to university. In other European countries, admittedly, students take longer to qualify and more of them fail. Some of those who obtain degrees from American universities would still not qualify for entry to Cambridge as undergraduates. Per head of population Britain has accumulated more Nobel prizes in physics than any other country. In terms of national economic achievement, however, it can be more rewarding to give many children some higher education than to ensure that a few receive the best. Because of their huge output of second class scientists and engineers, the United States have always been able to afford the cost of importing the first class men they have only recently begun to breed for themselves. In 1986, however, the Thatcher Government were still reducing their expenditure on British universities – by 2 per cent in real terms.

The deficiencies of British education constitute only one of the many explanations offered for Britain's decline. Because it was first advanced as a prediction, this theory is at least plausible, but it does not stand up well to the test of comparing contemporary British practice with earlier British experience. Education in Britain, for instance, may now be inadequate, but during the era of British economic supremacy it scarcely existed for most of the population.

The British class system is another factor often blamed for Britain's economic decline. Today it is certainly possible to argue – though the argument is often exaggerated by Britons who have never lived abroad – that British class distinctions are more conspicuous and have a more hereditary character than in other countries. It is harder to be sure what this argument proves. For a century Britain has become steadily more egalitarian at home and of less account abroad. The first process has certainly not gone as far as it could, but nor, more's the pity, has the second.

Many other causes have also been suggested for the decline of Britain. Adversary politics ranks with the archaic procedure of the House of Commons and the absence of managerial attitudes in the Civil Service. Those who do not blame the trade unions find scapegoats in the public schools. Some old-fashioned critics still denounce the influence of the classics and the churches. Engineers, it is generally agreed, are insufficiently esteemed in Britain. Becoming a country gentleman, so the envious have hinted, was a nationally unrewarding ambition. Losing an empire is said to have been as demoralising as having one was distracting. Prestige has been a snare and tradition a delusion. Some people even argue that the British, the English in particular, are congenitally idle. And the litter with which they desecrate every inhabited sector of their beautiful islands shows how much they lack the civic conscience of the Nordic peoples, of the Dutch or of the Swiss.

As criticisms of the British people and their social customs there is some truth in most of these charges. As explanations of Britain's decline they do not survive the two tests. Similar and often worse defects were apparent when Britain was at her international zenith and many of them can now be identified among her most successful rivals. In spite of the sixteen volumes which Arnold Toynbee devoted to the subject, some mystery still surrounds the nature of the virus which causes a nation, even a civilisation, to decay.

Many years have passed since it was possible for any but the boldest historians and students of political philosophy to visit the ruins of Baalbek. This is a pity, for there is no more visible proof of the extraordinary grandeur of the Roman Empire. Baalbek was once a remote, provincial staging-post for caravans, so insignificant a millenium and a half ago that Gibbon could find no mention of it by

The Scope for Change   153

any classical author. The battered remnants of its temple columns still dominate the Bekaa valley, matching the background dignity of snow-clad Lebanese mountains. The last vestiges of the Roman Empire vanished a thousand years ago and scholars still debate the cause.

There is thus no reason to expect the decline of Britain to be more readily explicable than that of the many ancient civilisations which have left their vast remains on the wind-swept heights of some Andean hill-side or buried in the depths of an Asian jungle. Not only do cultures come and go, but there are today many peoples, once far more potent and esteemed than those islanders in the North Sea, who have for centuries enjoyed no more than the half-life of national decay. There are also some who have actually managed to recover from their decline. No case is more striking, because none has a longer history, than that of China.

Could Britain still stage a comeback? Anyone who is superstitious about dates may like to remember that it was on 30 June 1688, towards the close of a century even more unfortunate for Britain than the twentieth has so far proved, that William of Orange was invited to come to England, to assume the crown and, as it turned out, to launch the British on their long ascent. Almost three centuries later 22 June 1988 will be the latest date for the next general election. Could that event conceivably inaugurate another Glorious Revolution?

It does not seem particularly likely. There is no obvious new leader waiting in the wings – as Dutch William was poised three centuries ago, or as Mao Tse Tung was ready forty years ago in China, or General de Gaulle thirty years ago in France. The selection will have to be made from the existing menu.

The Thatcher Government will be able to choose a date, whether in 1987 or in the first half of 1988, for confronting the electorate. If they get their timing right, they should have some arguments to put forward. The more volatile statistics – inflation, for instance, or the balance of payments – may present a hopeful contrast to the remorseless rise of crime or unemployment. With luck as well as judgement they may be able to avoid an urban riot or a major strike in the run-up to the general election. The mistakes of 1986 may have been forgotten and the disgruntled voters who then showed their resentment at by-elections may have returned to the fold. The Labour Party can be relied on for a few useful blunders and a third Conservative victory is quite conceivable.

But would it make much difference – in the long run? Those who strive for political impartiality can identify both achievements and failures in the record of Conservative administration since 1979. Partisans can support a variety of prejudices by careful choice of the years or the issues for comparison with what happened under previous governments. Rather more is required of anyone wishing to argue that two Thatcher governments have done enough to make it likely that a third would arrest or reverse the process of national decline. Recent statistics, as shown in Table 15.1, are not particularly reassuring.

Table 15.1 National statistics 1979–85

Year	1979	1980	1981	1982	1983	1984	1985
Homes built England & Wales	220722	213815	178859	157518	176988	184798	169257
Crimes ('000s) Ditto	2537	2688	2964	3262	3247	3499	3612
Unemployed % of workers	5.3	6.8	10.4	12.1	12.9	13.1	13.5
Energy used megatherms	61695	56537	54921	54279	54153	54052	56562
GDP at constant factor cost	103	100	98.3	100.1	103.1	106.4	110
Visible balance of trade (£million)	−3449	+1360	+3360	+2332	−836	−4391	−2068
Index of retail prices	223.5	263.7	295.0	320.4	335.1	351.8	373.2
	1979/80	1980/81	1981/82	1982/83	1983/84	1984/85	
Expenditure on education as % of GNP	5.1	5.5	5.4	5.4	5.3	5.1	

SOURCE: Central Statistical Office.

Only the regrettable figures – crime, unemployment and prices – show a consistently rising trend. Of course, unemployment increased during this period throughout the European Economic Community, but the British curve was always higher. A price had to be paid for this poor economic performance. In 1982 Britain, the pioneer of the National Health Service, lagged far behind both France and Germany in the numbers of doctors and of hospital beds per 1000 inhabitants. Where Britain still scored top marks was in the number of homes with baths and television sets.

To make sense statistics must be selected, a process which introduces an element of prejudice. A Conservative might choose other figures to give a better impression of Britain under Margaret Thatcher. Inflation, for instance, after an initial increase under

Conservative administration, fell to 3 per cent in April 1986, by which time it had altogether disappeared in Germany. It would not be difficult to draw favourable comparisons between the years of Conservative rule after 1979 and those of Labour government before that date. The best of Conservative propagandists would nevertheless find it hard to demonstrate either that Britain's decline had already been arrested or that another five years of the same medicine could confidently be expected to do the trick.

The obstacles faced by the parties of the Opposition are even greater. It is not difficult for them to denounce the government. So much really has gone wrong with Britain. The traditional industries, even those as essential to islanders as the merchant marine and shipbuilding, are decaying. The inner cities are crumbling. Oil will not last for ever and too much of it belongs, as do too many of the new factories, to foreigners. Fault-finding is no problem for the Opposition: a plausible programme for national reconstruction is another matter.

The severest critics of the two Thatcher governments can scarcely deny the novelty of some of their policies. If they failed, it was not because they shrank from change or clung to the tired consensus of earlier decades. Labour and the Alliance will find it hard to distance themselves from Conservative courses without falling back on measures that did not succeed last time they were tried. This need not prevent them from winning the election if the country is more inclined to vote the government out than to analyse the proposals of their rivals. There are already many electors with grievances: well over 3 million unemployed, for instance. The Conservatives could lose the next election – as Labour lost the elections of 1979 and 1983 – even if the alternative is less than convincing.

It is nevertheless likely that both Labour and the Alliance would have to buy votes with promises of increased expenditure: to create jobs, improve education, the National Health Service and welfare provisions; to house the homeless and to relieve distress. If implemented, such measures would tend both to increase inflation and to strain the balance of payments. The mere election of a government with that kind of programme would alarm international financiers. Any suggestion that the cost of expanding the economy and increasing social expenditure might be met from savings on defence would be resented by foreign governments.

Because of British membership of the European Economic Community and Mrs Thatcher's abolition of exchange controls, a new

Labour government would be even more vulnerable to international disapproval than was the Wilson administration in 1964. France, for instance, elected a Socialist President and parliamentary majority in 1981, but the pursuit of socialist policies encountered such international opposition that compromise soon became inescapable. And French socialists had started from an economic base stronger than anything Neil Kinnock would be likely to inherit.

It is naturally not certain that a Labour government with a clear majority would back down or seek help from the International Monetary Fund even if faced with a run on sterling and a flight of capital. The Labour Party has moved to the left and many of its members nowadays regard the compromises of the Wilson era as discreditable. Economic nationalism, even a siege economy, are conceivable reactions by a Labour government exposed to undue international pressure. The outcome would be unpredictable. So far, however, no proposals advanced by the Labour leadership have justified much hope that a Labour government would succeed where the Conservatives failed, and arrest Britain's decline.

That is a process which has gone on too long, has become a habit, a condition to which the British body politic has adapted itself. It would be an extraordinary election that would reverse a secular trend. Of course, the outcome of the election may well affect the pace of decline and vary the distribution among the British people of the consequences. That is how success for the Alliance might be significant. Their participation in a coalition government could moderate the ideological excesses of their Conservative or Socialist partners and help to smooth the downward path. It would take a more remarkable – and probably also a rougher – leader than anyone now visible to start the country on an uphill road.

In the twentieth century, however, elections have not been the major influence on the fate of Britain. The motive forces of fundamental change have usually had their origins abroad. The two world wars, the revolution in Russia, the turning against imperialism of the peoples of Asia and Africa: all these profoundly altered British political history. So, to a lesser extent, did the development of submarines, of aircraft, of nuclear weapons. The economic depression of the early thirties was an international phenomenon, more acutely felt in other countries than in Britain, but its repercussions still help to explain some features of British politics today.

Nuclear weapons might perhaps have appeared a little later without Lord Rutherford and the Cavendish Laboratory at Cambridge. Otherwise nobody in Britain initiated these developments and the

British governments that had to react to them had been elected earlier by voters with quite different preoccupations. To some extent politics has always been the art of coping with the unforeseen, but, in the later eighties, improvisation is more difficult than it used to be. Choice is also more restricted.

In 1914, for instance, and again in 1939 the British government of the day persuaded the House of Commons that Britain had no option. She had to go to war. In neither case was that strictly true. A minority took a different view at the time and hindsight makes it possible to argue that another decision might have been more prudent. Britain had not herself been attacked or injured. She could have held her fire.

Next time such arguments might simply be irrelevant. In 1986 fall-out from a minor nuclear accident at Chernobyl, deep in the Soviet Union, reached Britain. Even if some future British government were clever enough to avoid active participation in a nuclear war in Europe – which would not be easy, this might be insufficient to preserve most of the British people from the consequences of hundreds, perhaps even thousands, of nuclear explosions on the mainland. Opting out, however desirable, is unlikely to be possible.

Nevertheless, as earlier indicated, a change of government might bring changes in British foreign and defence policy that would at least vary, perhaps even reduce the risks to which Britain is now exposed. There are, for instance, over a hundred American military bases in Britain. It is arguable that these bases do more to make the British Isles a target for enemy attack than to provide Britain with any effective defence. Neutrality is probably not a feasible policy for Britain, but the French model – no foreign military bases on the national territory and no French forces committed to foreign command – has its attractions. American use of British airfields for their bombing raid on Libya in 1986 has made it more likely that such ideas will receive some consideration in the debate preceding the next general election.

One of the familiar precepts urged upon British politicians is: never say never. It is not a bad piece of advice even for writers on politics. British political history, to say nothing of the history of the world, has had to record so many surprising events during the twentieth century that it would be foolish to rule anything altogether out of the dozen years that remain. Of course there is still scope for major change, good as well as bad. That will be true until we reach what Lord Seafield described to the last Scottish parliament in 1707 as 'the end of an auld sang'.

The Renaissance of Britain is merely not very likely. The politicians now on the British stage are not men – or women – from whom achievements of heroic stature may reasonably be expected. They and leading Britons in other walks of life are not necessarily inferior in intelligence, education, virtue or general ability to most of their predecessors. If foreigners had not for many years visibly been doing better for themselves, it would be hard to argue that the British people had deteriorated. If a miracle-worker were to appear, the clay would not be lacking for him to mould. He would still find it difficult.

Late twentieth-century Britons can no longer expect some of the things their ancestors took for granted. The world has changed too much to allow Britons to dream of regaining the independence the Victorians enjoyed. The British Isles will remain vulnerable to enemy attack and the British economy precariously viable. It is not certain that Britain will continue to decline by comparison with other advanced nations, but it is likely. Events since the Second World War suggest that even another disaster that spared Britain, but struck down her rivals, might not suffice to reverse the trend. Political change within Britain could, however, speed up or retard the process. It could vary the distribution among the British people of the material consequences of national decline. Nations, no less than human beings, can also go downhill with rather different degrees of dignity.

On 23 May 1986, for instance, the British Prime Minister, disturbed by the likely economic repercussions of a fall in the number of American tourists visiting Britain, made a remarkable broadcast to the United States.

> Please come, . . . Please change your mind. Not only does it help our standard of living and our economy, but we miss you. We like seeing you. We love your friendliness. We love your warmth. We love your generosity and we are missing it on our streets.

For her American listeners these words probably had more appeal than any briskly statistical reminder that they were 17 times more likely to be murdered in the United States than in England and Wales. Only British ears ached at the mendicant note.

Of course, King James II sometimes struck that jarring chord in his frequent applications to the French Ambassador for financial assistance from King Louis XIV. For nearly three centuries, however, it had not been heard from a British government. Even in the dark February of 1941 Churchill had told Roosevelt: 'give us the tools and we will finish the job'.

That was another time than this.

Bibliography

Published Sources and Suggestions for Further Reading

General

BAGEHOT, WALTER (1983) *The English Constitution*, with introduction by R. M. S. Crossman, (Fontana Classics, 17th Impression, London).
BUTLER, DAVID and KAVANAGH, DENNIS (1984) *The British General Election of 1983* (Macmillan, London).
BUTLER, DAVID and BUTLER, GARETH (1986) *British Political Facts 1900–1985* (6th edn) (Macmillan, London).
CENTRAL OFFICE OF INFORMATION, *Britain 1987* (published annually) *An Official Handbook* (HMSO, London).
CENTRAL STATISTICAL OFFICE (1980) *Facts in Focus* (5th edn) (Penguin, Harmondsworth and HMSO, London).
CENTRAL STATISTICAL OFFICE
 Annual Abstract of Statistics
 Economic Trends (monthly)
 Monthly Digest of Statistics
 National Income and Expenditure (annual)
 Social Trends (annual) – (all HMSO, London).
DRUCKER, HENRY (1983) (ed.) *Developments in British Politics* (Macmillan, London).
JONES, BILL and KAVANAGH, DENNIS (1983) *British Politics Today* (2nd edn) (Manchester University Press).
LEYS, COLIN (1983) *Politics in Britain: An Introduction* (Heinemann Educational Books Ltd, London).
MORAN, MICHAEL (1985) *Politics and Society in Britain* (Macmillan, London).
OSMAN, TONY (1985) *The Facts of Everyday Life* (Faber & Faber, London).
ROSE, RICHARD (1980) *Politics in England* (Little, Brown, Boston).
SAMPSON, ANTHONY (1982) *The Changing Anatomy of Britain* (Hodder & Stoughton, London).
TAYLOR, A. J. P. (1979) *English History 1914–1945* (Pelican Books, London).
THE TIMES (daily) London.
TOCH, HENRY (1983) *Essentials of British Constitution and Government* (Cassell, London).

1 Introduction

BENN, TONY (1982) *Parliament, People and Power* (Verso, London).
BROWN, ARCHIE and KASER, MICHAEL (1982) *Soviet Policy for the 1980s* (Macmillan, London).
KELLNER, PETER and HITCHENS, CHRISTOPHER (1976) *Callaghan: The road to Number Ten* (Cassell, London).
NORTON, PHILIP (1982) *The Constitution in Flux* (Martin Robertson, Oxford).
SAMPSON (1982).
SCOTT, JOHN (1982) *The Upper Classes* (Macmillan, London).
VOSLENSKY, MICHAEL (1984) *Nomenklatura: Anatomy of the Soviet Ruling Class* (The Bodley Head, London).
WHO'S WHO } (Adam & Charles Black, London),
WHO WAS WHO } various years.

2 Absence of a Written Constitution

BENN (1982).
BIRCH, ANTHONY H. (1982) *The British System of Government* (5th edn) (George Allen & Unwin, London).
BUTLER, DAVID (1983) *Governing Without a Majority* (William Collins, London).
GUINNESS BOOK OF RECORDS (1985) (Guinness Superlatives, London).
HARVEY, J. and BATHER L. (1977) *The British Constitution* (Macmillan, London).
NICOLSON, HAROLD (1952) *King George The Fifth* (Constable, London).
NORTON (1982).
NORTON-TAYLOR, RICHARD (1985) *The Ponting Affair* (Cecil Woolf, London).
NOY, MICHAEL de la (1985) *The Honours System* (Alison & Busby, London).
ROYAL COMMISSION ON THE CONSTITUTION 1969–1973 (HMSO London, October 1973 Cmnd 5460).
TREVELYAN, G. M. (1930–34) *England Under Queen Anne* (3 vols) (Longmans, Green, London).
—— (1920) *Lord Grey of the Reform Bill* (Longmans, Green, London).
WHEELER-BENNETT, JOHN W. (1958) *King George VI* (Macmillan, London).
WILSON, HAROLD (1979) *Final Term: The Labour Government 1974–1976* (Weidenfeld & Nicolson and Michael Joseph, London).
WOLF-PHILLIPS, LESLIE (1984) 'A long look at the British constitution' in *Parliamentary Affairs* Autumn.

3 The Executive in Britain

BAGEHOT (1983).
BENN (1982).

Bibliography and Further Reading 161

BUTLER (1983).
BUTLER & KAVANAGH (1984).
FALKENDER, LADY MARCIA (1983) *Downing Street in Perspective* (Weidenfeld & Nicholson, London).
GORE-BOOTH, LORD (ed.) (1979) *Satow's Guide to Diplomatic Practice* (5th edn) (Longman Group, London).
HARVEY (1977).
HURD, DOUGLAS (1979) *An End to Promises: Sketch of a Government 1970-74* (Collins, London).
KING, ANTHONY (ed.) (1985) *The British Prime Minister* (2nd edn) (Macmillan, London).
WEINSTEIN, EDWIN A. (1981) *Woodrow Wilson: A Medical and Psychological Biography* (Princeton University Press, Princeton, New Jersey).
WHITELEY, PAUL (1983) *The Labour Party in Crisis* (Methuen, London).
WILSON, HAROLD (1971) *The Labour Government 1964-1970* (Weidenfeld & Nicolson and Michael Joseph, London).
—— (1976) *The Governance of Britain* (Weidenfeld & Nicolson and Michael Joseph, London).
WILSON (1979).

4 Legitimacy

BAGEHOT (1983).
BUTLER (1983).
BUTLER (1984).
BUTLER (1986).
NICOLSON (1952).
NORTON (1982).
STRACHEY, LYTTON (1921) *Queen Victoria* (Chatto & Windus, London).
WHEELER-BENNETT (1958).
WILSON (1979).

5 How Cabinet and Commons Operate

BENN, TONY (1981) *Arguments for Democracy*, ed. Chris Mullin (Jonathan Cape, London).
CASTLE, BARBARA (1980) *The Castle Diaries 1974-76* (Weidenfeld & Nicolson, London).
FALKENDER (1983).
GOWING, MARGARET (1974) *Independence and Deterrence: Britain and Atomic Energy 1945-1952* Vol. I (Macmillan, London).
HARVEY (1977).
HOWARD, ANTHONY (ed.) (1979) *The Crossman Diaries: Selections from The Diaries of a Cabinet Minister 1964-1970* (Hamish Hamilton and Jonathan Cape, London).
HURD (1979).
KING (1985).

LLOYD, SELWYN (1977) *Mr. Speaker, Sir* (Readers Union, Newton Abbot).
NORTON (1982).
ROSKILL, STEPHEN (1972) *Hankey: Man of Secrets Vol II 1919–1931* (Collins, London).
SAMPSON (1982).
WHEELER-BENNETT (1958).
YOUNG, G. M. (1952) *Stanley Baldwin* (Rupert Hart-Davis, London).

6 The Servants of the State

BAGEHOT (1983).
BENN (1981).
CASTLE (1980).
FALKENDER (1983).
GREENWOOD, JOHN and WILSON DAVID (1984) *Public Administration in Britain* (George Allen & Unwin, London).
HOWARD (1979).
HURD (1979).
KISSINGER, HENRY (1979) *The White House Years* (Weidenfeld & Nicolson and Michael Joseph, London).
LEYS (1983).
MACRAE, STUART and PITT, DOUGLAS (1980) *Public Administration: an introduction* (Pitman Publishing, London).
MOORHOUSE, GEOFFREY (1977) *The Diplomats* (Jonathan Cape, London).
MORAN (1985).
NICOLSON (1952).
ORWELL, GEORGE (1947) *The English People* (Collins, London).
WILSHER, PETER; MACINTYRE, DONALD; and JONES, MICHAEL (1985) *Strike* (Coronet Books, London).

7 The Rivals of the State

BAGEHOT (1983).
CHAPPLE, FRANK (1984) *Sparks Fly: A Trade Union Life* (Michael Joseph, London).
DEPARTMENT OF EMPLOYMENT (1986) *Employment Gazette* (London, January).
GORMLEY, JOE (1982) *Battered Cherub* (Hamish Hamilton, London).
GREENWOOD (1984).
JONES, NICHOLAS (1984) *Strikes and the Media* (Basil Blackwell, Oxford).
PIMLOTT, BEN and COOK, CHRIS (1982) *Trade Unions in British Politics* (Longman Group, London).
TAYLOR, ROBERT (1982) *Workers and the New Depression* (Macmillan, London).
TUNSTALL, JEREMY (1983) *The Media in Britain* (Constable, London).
WILSHER (1985).

8 The Commonwealth

BARNETT, CORRELLI (1972) *The Collapse of British Power* (Methuen, London).
JUDD, DENIS and SLINN, PETER (1982) *The Evolution of the Modern Commonwealth 1902–80* (Macmillan, London).
KENNEDY, PAUL (1984) essay 'Why did the British Empire Last so Long?' in *Strategy and Diplomacy 1870–1945* (Fontana, London).
MILLER, J. D. B. (1978) *Survey of Commonwealth Affairs 1953–69* (Oxford University Press).
OWEN, DAVID (1978) *Human Rights* (Jonathan Cape, London).
SUPPERSTONE, MICHAEL and LAING, ELISABETH (1983) *Immigration: the Law and Practice* (Oyez Longman, London).
WOODRUFF (MASON), PHILIP (1954) *The Men Who Ruled India: The Guardians* (Jonathan Cape, London).

9 Parties and Factions

BEITH, ALAN (1983) *The Case for the Liberal Party and the Alliance* (Longmans, London)
BENN (1982).
BLAKE, ROBERT (1985) *The Conservative Party from Peel to Thatcher* (Methuen, London).
BUTLER (1983).
BUTLER (1984).
BUTLER (1986).
CHURCHILL, WINSTON (1948) *The Gathering Storm* (Cassell, London).
DROWER, G. M. F. (1984) *Neil Kinnock: The Path to Leadership* (Weidenfeld & Nicolson, London).
HEATH, ANTHONY; JOWELL, ROGER and CURTICE, JOHN (1985) *How Britain Votes* (Pergamon, London).
HOLMES, MARTIN (1985) *The First Thatcher Government 1979–1983* (Wheatsheaf Books, Brighton).
JOHNSON, R. W. (1985) *The Politics of Recession* (Macmillan, London).
JOSEPHS, JEREMY (1983) *Inside the Alliance* (John Martin, London).
NICOLSON (1952).
NOY (1985).
OWEN, DAVID (1984) *A Future That Will Work* (Penguin, Harmondsworth).
—— (1986) *A United Kingdom* (Penguin, Harmondsworth).
PELLING, HENRY (1985) *A Short History of the Labour Party* (8th edn) (Macmillan, London).
PIMLOTT (1982).
PYM, FRANCIS (1984) *The Politics of Consent* (Hamish Hamilton, London).
ROBERTSON, DAVID (1984) *Class and the British Electorate* (Basil Blackwell, Oxford).
SHIPLEY, PETER (1983) *The Militant Tendency: Trotskyism in the Labour Party* (Foreign Affairs Publishing Co., Richmond).

STEPHENSON, HUGH (1982) *Claret and Chips: The Rise of the SDP* (Michael Joseph, London).
WHITELEY (1983).
YOUNG, HUGO and SLOMAN, ANNE (1986) *The Thatcher Phenomenon* (British Broadcasting Corporation, London).

10 Divisions on Constitutional Issues

BENN (1981).
BENN (1982).
LLOYD GEORGE, DAVID (1938) *War Memoirs* (Odhams Press, London).
NORTON (1982).
OWEN (1984).
OWEN (1986).

11 Divisions on Economic and Social Policy

ALT, J. (1979) *The Politics of Economic Decline* (Cambridge University Press).
CAVES, RICHARD E. and KRAUSE, LAWRENCE, B. (1980) *Britain's Economic Performance* (The Brookings Institution, Washington).
GAMBLE, ANDREW (1985) *Britain in Decline* (2nd edn) (Macmillan, London).
GAMBLE, A. M. and WALKLAND, S. A. (1984) *The British Party System and Economic Policy 1945–1983* (Clarendon Press, Oxford).
HOLMES (1985).
HOUSE OF LORDS (1985) Report from the Select Committee on Overseas Trade (HMSO, London) 30 July.
KIRBY, M. W. (1981) *The Decline of British Economic Power Since 1870* (George Allen & Unwin, London).
POLLARD, SIDNEY (1982) *The Wasting of the British Economy* (Croom Helm, London).
SMITH, KEITH (1984) *The British Economic Crisis* (Penguin, Harmondsworth).

12 Divisions on Foreign and Defence Policy

BARNETT (1972).
BARNETT, CORRELLI (1986) *The Audit of War: The Illusion and Reality of Britain as a Great Nation* (Macmillan, London).
BAYLIS, JOHN (1984) *Anglo-American Defence Relations 1939–84* (Macmillan, London).
CABLE, JAMES (1983) *Britain's Naval Future* (Macmillan, London).
—— (1985) *Diplomacy at Sea* (Macmillan, London).
CAMPBELL, DUNCAN (1984) *The Unsinkable Aircraft Carrier: American Military Bases in Britain* (Michael Joseph, London).

Bibliography and Further Reading 165

CLARKE, MAGNUS (1982) *The Nuclear Destruction of Britain* (Croom Helm, London).
CYR, ARTHUR (1979) *British Foreign Policy and the Atlantic Area* (Macmillan, London).
GOWING (1974).
HOLMES (1985).
JOHNSON, PETER (1985) *Neutrality: A Policy for Britain* (Temple Smith, London).
JUDD (1982).
MARWICK, ARTHUR (1968) *Britain in the Century of Total War* (The Bodley Head, London).
PARTY PAMPHLETS:
 Conservative Research Department *Defence* 15 September 1986
 Labour Party – *Defence and security for Britain* 1984
  Defence Conversion and Costs 1986
 SDP-Liberal Alliance – *Defence and Disarmament* June 1986
SECRETARY OF STATE FOR DEFENCE STATEMENT ON THE DEFENCE ESTIMATES (annual) (HMSO, London).
SIMPSON, JOHN (1983) *The Independent Nuclear State: The United States, Britain and the Military Atom* (Macmillan, London).
SMITH, DAN (1980) *The Defence of the Realm in the 1980s* (Croom Helm, London).
SUNDAY TIMES INSIGHT TEAM (1982) *The Falklands War* (Sphere Books, London).
THOMPSON, E. P. and SMITH, DAN (1980) *Protest and Survive* (Penguin, Harmondsworth).
WALLACE, WILLIAM (1984) *Britain's Bilateral Links Within Western Europe* (Routledge & Kegan Paul, London).
—— (1975) *The Foreign Policy Process in Britain* (RIIA, London)
WILSON (1971).
WILSON (1979).

13 The Special Problem of Ulster

ALEXANDER, YONAH and O'DAY, ALAN (1984) *Terrorism in Ireland* (Croom Helm, Beckenham).
BELL, GEOFFREY (1984) *The British in Ireland: A Suitable Case for Withdrawal* (Pluto Press, London).
BEW, PAUL and PATTERSON, HENRY (1985) *The British State and the Ulster Crisis* (Verso, London).
CENTRAL OFFICE OF INFORMATION (1978) *Northern Ireland* (C.O.I., London).
COOGAN, TIM PAT (1971) *The IRA* (Fontana, London).
HAMILL, DESMOND (1985) *Pig in the Middle: The Army in Northern Ireland 1969–1984* (Methuen, London).
KEE, ROBERT (1973) *The Green Flag* (Weidenfeld & Nicolson, London).
MACAULAY, LORD (1967) *History of England* (Heron Books, London).
MORAN (1985).

MOXON-BROWNE, EDWARD (1983) *Nation, Class and Creed in Northern Ireland* (Gower, Aldershot).
SUNDAY TIMES INSIGHT TEAM (1972) *Ulster* (Penguin, Harmondsworth).
TAYLOR (1979).
WATT, DAVID (ed.) (1981) *The Constitution of Northern Ireland* (Heinemann, London).

14 Civil Liberties in Britain

COOK, JUDITH (1985) *The Price of Freedom* (New English Library, London).
HEWITT, PATRICIA (1982) *The Abuse of Power: Civil Liberties in the United Kingdom* (Martin Robertson, Oxford).
LILLY, MARK (1984) *The National Council for Civil Liberties: The First Fifty Years* (Macmillan, London).
MILL, JOHN STUART (1936) *On Liberty* (J. M. Dent, London) (first published 1859).
NORTON, PHILIP (ed.) (1984) *Law and Order and British Politics* (Gower, Aldershot).
OWEN (1978).
PEARSON, GEOFFREY (1983) *Hooligan: A History of Respectable Fears* (Macmillan, London).
TAYLOR (1979).

15 The Scope for Change

ARCHER, DANE and GARTNER, ROSEMARY (1984) *Violence and Crime in Cross-National Perspective* (Yale University Press).
BARNETT (1986).
DAICHES, DAVID (1977) *Scotland and the Union* (John Murray, London).
ECONOMIST, The (1984) The World in Figures (London).
GAMBLE (1981).
GIBBON, EDWARD (1875) *Decline and Fall of the Roman Empire* (Chatto & Windus, London) (first published 1788).
JOHNSON (1985).
KENNEDY, PAUL (1980) *The Rise of the Anglo-German Antagonism 1860–1914* (George Allen & Unwin, London).
KURIAN, G. T. (1979) *The Book of World Rankings* (Macmillan, London).
MACAULAY (1967).
MATTHEWS, R. C. O.; FEINSTEIN, C. H.; and ODLING SMEE, J. C. (1982) *British Economic Growth 1856–1973* (Clarendon Press, Oxford).
MITCHELL, B. R. (1971) *Abstract of British Historical Statistics* (Cambridge University Press).
—— (1981) *European Historical Statistics 1750–1975* (Macmillan, London).
PLAYFAIR, LYON (1889) *Subjects of Social Welfare* (Cassell, London).

SHOWERS, VICTOR (1979) *World Facts and Figures* (John Wiley and Sons, New York).
TOCQUEVILLE, ALEXIS de (1951) *De la Démocratie en Amérique* (Gallimard, Paris).
TOYNBEE, ARNOLD (1935–59) *A Study of History* (Oxford University Press).
UNITED NATIONS (1985) *Statistical Yearbook for 1982* (United Nations, New York).

Index

Africa 12, 82–3, 121, 151
Alliance of Liberals & Social Democrats
  candidates 93
  consensus 104
  & coalition 37, 96, 117
  & Community 115
  constitutional ideas 16, 41, 99, 103–4, 107
  devolution 104
  economic policy 114–17
  electoral record 40, 91
  & foreign policy 125, 128
  leaders 16, 91–2, 96
  proportional representation 91–2, 96, 99, 103–4
  prospects 91–2, 117, 155–6
  tough and tender 114
Andropov, Yuri (1914–84): Soviet leader 7
Argentina (*see also* Falklands) 123
Armed forces
  British 5, 27–30, 52, 56–8, 62, 65, 69, 82–3, 102, 119–20, 126–8, 143
  foreign 57–8, 143
  ministerial control 5, 62
  recruitment 57–8, 62, 82, 118, 131
Asia 86, 153, 156
Asquith, Herbert, later Earl of Oxford and Asquith (1852–1928): British Prime Minister 13, 15, 37, 87
Attlee, Clement, later Earl (1883–1967): British Prime Minister 26, 47, 81, 97, 118
Australia
  & Britain 83, 120
  constitutional practice 15, 49, 58, 80
  dominion 78–9
  monarchy 80

Bagehot, Walter (1826–77): British writer 28, 34–6, 40, 53, 61, 76
Baldwin, Stanley, later Earl Baldwin of Bewdley: British Prime Minister 17, 45, 98
Belize 83
Benn, Tony, formerly Lord Stansgate (1925–): British politician
  & 'Absolute Premiership' 25
  & civil service 59
  & constitutional change 104
  left wing leader 5–6
  peerage of 5, 13
  suggests creating peers 13
Bevin, Ernest (1881–1951): British Foreign Secretary 3, 89
Bonar Law, Andrew (1858–1923): British Prime Minister 37, 87
Brezhnev, Leonid (1906–82): Soviet leader 7
British Constitution
  Act of Settlement 14, 32–3
  advantages & disadvantages 12–21, 39
  Bagehot on 28, 34–6, 76
  Bill of Rights 14, 99, 140
  changes in 15–21, 35, 41, 61, 75–6, 98–100, 104, 106–7
  character of 12–21, 40, 54, 99
  & EEC 104
  effective & dignified parts 34–8, 55, 77, 81
  emergency legislation 17, 29
  flexibility 18–20, 106
  foreign constraints 106–7
  importance of precedent 12–21, 37
  independence & sovereignty 10, 15, 121–3, 126–7, 158
  living organism 21, 43
  nationality 15, 84–6
  pious fictions of 43

British Constitution – *continued*
  as political issue 99–107
  powers of Prime Minister 23, 27, 32, 43
  proportional representation 37, 41, 99–100, 103–4
  & royal prerogative 28–9, 32, 35–8, 81
  uncertainty of 12–21, 23–32, 37, 100, 140
  use of plebiscites 18–20, 92–3, 99
British economy
  balance of payments & trade 111–12, 115, 153–6
  compared with others 111–13, 150–1, 154–6, 158
  decline 79, 81, 85, 88–9, 98, 103–4, 107–10, 112–13, 115–17, 124, 146, 150–6, 158
  industry 111–12, 114, 149–51, 155
  inflation 110–13, 115–17, 153–5
  investment 110, 112
  issues 108–17, 155–6
  monetarism 110–11
  & multinational corporations 72–3
  New Economic Strategy 104, 106, 110
  oil 19, 112, 115, 122, 124, 155
  policy 10, 83–4, 88–90, 94, 101, 103–4, 106–7, 110–17, 119, 121, 156
  & productivity 111–12
  real incomes 109, 149–51
  rise of 148–9
  statistics 153–4
  & Thatcher government 75, 94, 101, 104, 107, 111–17, 153–5
  & trade unions 70, 88–90
  & Treasury 22
  & unemployment 88, 94, 101, 104, 109–17, 146–7, 150, 153–6
  wages 110–11
  what went wrong? 151–3
British Empire
  decolonisation 78–9, 84–5, 119–21, 123
  dominions 77
  extent of 9, 78, 82, 119, 148
  Imperial Conference of 1926 77–8
  influence on British politics 9, 62, 79, 81, 119–21, 152
  nature of 77–8, 81, 84–5
  net military burden 83
  prestige 78, 81
British government (*see also* Cabinet)
  centralised character 55, 62–3, 101
  & civil service 56–62, 65
  constraints on 10, 51, 54–5, 75, 89–90, 102, 155–6
  cult of secrecy 47–9, 53, 55, 61, 101
  described 22–32, 44–55, 64–5, 73, 76, 102
  fall of 43–4, 52
  Home Office 22, 62, 102
  mendicant 158
  must react to unforeseen 157
  National of 1931 37
  secrets withheld 48
British politics (*see also* Defence, Foreign Policy, *etc.*)
  adversarial character 54, 92, 98, 103, 152
  alternative action 105–6, 147
  change in 7–11, 58, 60, 90, 98, 103–7, 145, 148–58
  chauvinism 85–6, 95, 107, 145–7
  continuity in 8, 59–60, 89, 120
  decentralisation 19, 99, 104
  geography of 88, 94, 111–12
  Green Party 97
  ideology in 6
  influence of public opinion 18, 42, 83–6, 88, 92, 96, 103, 117, 119–28
  international context of 9–10, 81, 89, 106, 118–28, 148–58
  law & order 88, 94, 101–3, 105–6, 116, 133, 135–8, 153–4
  nationalism in 93–4, 96–7, 114, 122–5, 127–8
  parties & factions in 87–98

British Politics – *continued*
  patriotism 88, 158
  pragmatism 120
  pressure groups 97
  racialism in 86, 94–5, 145–7
  religion in 75, 139
  republicanism 34, 36
  revolutionaries in 37, 65, 95–8
  Scottish nationalism in 19, 42, 94, 96–7
  separation of powers 45–6, 50–5, 75
  unemployment as issue 88, 94, 101, 117, 128, 146, 153–5
  Vietnam issue 46, 118, 122
  volatile 7
British society
  expectation of life 113
  general 8–9, 38, 65, 75, 88, 90, 92, 104
  housing 11, 113, 146, 154–5
  issues 115–17, 145–7
  quality of life 109, 154
  social reform 10, 89–90
  social services 112, 116–17, 155
  stability 8–10
Burma 80, 84, 119
Butler, David (1924–): British writer, *Governing Without a Majority* 37

Cabinet
  Cabinet Office 47–9, 100
  collective authority 22–7
  collective responsibility 23–5
  committees of 47, 49
  composition 22, 45, 47
  delegates authority 49–50
  & House of Commons 22–3, 30–2, 40, 45, 50–5
  meeting-place 45–6
  operation of 46–51
  & party 30–2, 50
  power of 22–6
  & Prime Minister 22, 32, 43–4, 46–54, 99
  & Queen's Speech 36
  Secretary 16, 48, 59–61

solidarity of 18, 47
treason absolved in 87
Callaghan, James (1912–): British Prime Minister 5, 19, 26–7, 43, 48, 52, 118, 155
Cambridge
  Greek evening in 147
  International Summer School at viii
  MP for 93
  Rutherford at 156
  Trinity College 23
  university of 6, 8, 151
Canada
  citizenship 84
  Conservatives in 87
  constitutional practice 15, 49, 68, 80
  dominion 78
  & labour disputes 68–9
  unemployment 112
Capital
  concentrations of 73, 144
  defence of 87–8
  expiring 110
  flight of 156
  funds for Conservative Party 97
  political influence of 104, 107
  & property 64, 87–8, 90
Carrington, Lord (1919–): British Foreign Secretary 3, 16
Carson, Sir Edward, later Lord (1854–1935): British politician 87
Ceausescu, Nicolae (1918–): Romanian leader 4
Centurion in New Testament 2
Chamberlain, Neville (1869–1940): British Prime Minister 30–1, 52, 148
Channel Islands 33
Chernenko, Konstantin (1911–85): Soviet leader 7
Chile 123
China 150, 153
Churches in Britain 22–3, 38, 66, 75–6, 152
Churchill, Winston, later Sir (1874–1965): British Prime Minister 25–6, 31, 81, 98, 158

Index

Civil liberties
  abridgement of 17
  Bill of Rights 99, 140
  in Britain 139–47
  & Conservative Party 139
  freedom of information 99–101
  Habeas Corpus 140–2
  human rights 99, 105, 139–40
  & Left 139
  & Liberal Party 96, 139
  more enemies than State 145
  National Council for 143
  opinions 143–4
  passports 28, 141
  Prevention of Terrorism Act 140–1
  priority of 108
  & racialism 145–7
  religious toleration 139
  & Security 140
  & Ulster 132
  violence 68–71, 102–3, 140, 144, 147
Civil Service
  autonomous power 49, 57, 61–2, 65, 122
  & Cabinet Office 48–50
  criticism of 58–62, 65, 104, 152
  disaffection of 102
  duties of 56–62, 122–3
  ethos 59–62, 123, 125
  ministerial control 22, 49, 60–2
  pay 31, 102
  permanently employed 56
  Permanent Secretaries & Under-Secretaries 53–4, 59, 61
  & trade unions 69
  unpolitical 56–8, 60, 64
Class (*see also* Governing class)
  bias 64, 141
  gentlemen 9, 88, 152
  influence 88, 90, 152
  middle 91, 141, 143
  upper 143
  working 3, 88–92, 143
Coalition
  in Finland 87
  government 32, 37, 44, 52, 87, 104
  Prime Minister in 26, 32
  principle of 16, 96
Commonwealth
  advantages 81, 83–4
  & British political system 77, 79–86, 121
  & Crown 77–82
  dependencies 78–9, 84, 123
  described 77–86
  dignified part of constitution 77–81, 123
  & Empire 77–9, 81–5
  extent 78, 82
  governors-general 79
  Heads of Government 78, 83
  immigration 84–6, 94, 145–7
  international status 82
  other monarchs 78
  & Queen Elizabeth II 77–82
  republics in 78, 80
  & sanctions 81, 83
  & trade 83–4
Communist Party
  British 5, 67, 95–6, 142
  of Soviet Union 3–4, 6, 95
Consensus
  & Alliance 104
  & change 103–7, 155
  & Commonwealth 82
  defence & foreign policy 120, 128
  disappearance of 10, 102, 117, 128
Conservative Party (British)
  & bureaucracy 49, 65
  & coalition 37
  choice of leader 15–17, 93
  composition 5, 87–8, 90, 92, 94
  constitutional ideas 16, 87, 99–104, 107
  defence 118, 126–8
  deference 31
  economic policy 88, 94, 101, 103–4, 107, 110–17, 153–6
  & EEC 18, 110, 121, 124–5
  electoral record 26, 36–7, 40–2, 88–9, 92
  factions 94
  ideology 88, 101–4, 156

Conservative Party – *continued*
  & media 74
  money 94, 97–8
  & overseas policy 120–8
  Party chairman 50
  proper name 87
  prospects 92, 117, 153
  revolts 31–2, 87
  & trade unions 67, 88, 101, 122
  & Ulster 130–1, 136–7
Constitution (*see also* British Constitution)
  entrenchment 14
  Finnish 14–15
  French 12, 34, 58, 75
  German 34, 49, 68
  republican 34
  secession 20, 79
  under pressure 106
  unwritten 12–21, 100
  US 12, 14–15, 27–8, 38, 42, 49, 51, 53–4, 58, 73, 75, 100
  written 12, 100
Crossman, Richard (1907–1974): British politician 23–4, 46, 48–9, 61
Crown (British)
  & Commonwealth 77–82
  & constitution 23, 27–9, 33, 81
  dependencies 33
  & Protestant religion 33
Curzon, Lord (1859–1925): British politician 17, 32
Czechoslovakia 82, 126

Defence policy
  American military bases 127–8, 157
  British 6, 10, 48, 62, 79, 82, 92, 96, 108, 121, 126–8
  Chiefs of Staff 119
  Conservative 118, 122–3, 126–8
  Labour 118, 122–3, 126–8, 155, 157
  & NATO 125–6, 128
  overseas bases 119
  political importance of 128, 156
  Royal Navy 65
  tail wags dog 121, 127

Diplomats
  ambassadors 27–8, 65
  commissions 27, 65
  duties of viii, 56
  social origins 65
  unpolitical 56–7
Douglas-Home, Sir Alec (*see also* Home, Earl of) (1903–): British Prime Minister 6, 45, 93
Dulles, J. F. (1888–1959): US Secretary of State 5

Eden, Sir Anthony, later Earl of Avon (1897–1977): British Prime Minister 26–7, 31, 118
Education
  British 4, 9, 101, 116–17, 151–2, 154
  & governing class 4–6, 9, 65, 88–91
  Inspectors' report 151
  neglect of 151, 154
  & parties 92, 101, 104, 151, 155
  public schools 9, 152
  teachers strike 116
  university 151
Eisenhower, Dwight D. (1890–1969): US President 5
European countries
  comparisons with 57–8, 64, 85, 97–8, 108–9, 112–13, 119, 121
  Council of Europe 105
  European Defence Policy 122, 126
  European Foreign Policy 122, 126
  European Free Trade Area 121
  year of Europe 122
European Economic Community (EEC)
  & British independence 15, 104, 106–7
  British membership 18, 24, 49, 84, 90, 107, 110, 121–6, 128, 155
  Commission 125
  Community law 105
  Council of Ministers 125

Index

European Economic
   Community – *continued*
   Court of Justice 105
   distrust of 114–15, 121, 124–5
   European Parliament 125
   federalism 122
   political & military dimension 126
   power of 73, 124
   unemployment in 154
   withdrawal from 128

Falklands War of 1982 24, 74, 79, 83, 88, 117, 120, 123
Finland 14–15, 53, 58, 85, 87, 97
First World War
   Anglo-French staff talks before 24
   British options 157
   economic consequences 108, 150, 156
   Irish trouble before 87
   & Liberal Party 89, 91
Foot, Michael (1913–): British politician 26, 90
Foreign policy
   British 6, 10, 59, 61, 89, 118–28
   Conservative 118, 120–8
   Foreign Office 22, 35, 59, 61, 102, 119
   Foreign Secretaries 3, 16, 27–8, 61, 85, 89, 118
   Labour 118, 121–3, 127–8
   & NATO 125–6, 128
   political importance of 128
   prestige 127
   & royal prerogative 28–9, 35
   & US 118–23, 126–8
France
   & Algeria 14, 82, 85, 121
   & Britain 84, 106, 112, 121, 153–4, 157–8
   Code Napoléon 64
   constitution 12, 34, 58, 75
   & defence 157
   & EEC 121
   & Germany 126
   & Indochina 82, 121
   legislators 53
   media in 74
   presidents of 24, 102, 156
   revolution 8, 17
   riots 102, 106
   suicide in 109
   trade unions 66

Gaulle, Charles de (1890–1970): French President 34, 102, 121–2, 153
General elections
   Boundary Commission 41
   constituencies 41–3
   deposit required of candidates 42
   expenditure 97
   franchise 13, 15, 41–2, 88, 91–2
   future 16–17, 36–7, 117, 128, 153, 155–7
   1906 91
   1923 37
   1935 31, 41
   1945 26
   1951 26, 41
   Feb 1974 19, 36, 41, 44, 68, 91
   Oct 1974 19
   1979 19, 26, 40, 90, 109–11, 117, 155
   1983 19, 26, 40, 90–2, 94–5, 97, 117, 125, 155
   preparations for 59
   Prime Minister chooses date of 23, 30, 32, 153
   proportional representation 37, 40–1, 91–2, 96, 99, 103–4
   & royal prerogative 29
   safe seats 42–3
Germany
   British relations with 119–20, 126–7, 150–1
   comparisons with 82, 85, 106, 108, 112, 121, 142, 150–1, 154–5
   constitutional practice 49, 68
   & Hitler 4
   & Ireland 131, 134
   & NATO 126
   rearmament of 126
   suicide in 109
   trade with 73, 151

Gibbon, Edward (1737–94): British historian 152
Gibraltar 79, 83, 85, 98
Gorbachev, Mikhail (1931–): Soviet leader 7, 54
Governing class
 apprenticeship 5–6
 assembly of 44
 British 4–10, 21, 65, 87, 89–91, 106
 change in 6–11, 144
 concept explained 2
 constraints on 7, 10
 distinguished from ruling class 3
 & Empire 79
 entry to 5–6, 9, 42, 57, 65, 93
 favourite slogan 21
 ideology in 6–7, 64–5
 in Romania 4
 in Soviet Union 3–8
 in United States 4–5, 7–8, 58, 65
 & wealth 5, 9
Greece 69, 119
Grenada 80
Grey, Lord (1764–1845): British Prime Minister 13–14, 17
Guatemala 123

Healey, Denis (1917–): British politician 119
Heath, Edward (1916–): British Prime Minister 18, 36, 68, 70, 109, 115, 122
Hitler, Adolf (1889–1945): German leader 4, 34
Home, Earl of (*see also* Douglas-Home) 6, 16
Hong Kong 79, 123
House of Commons
 agenda 22, 50–1
 & budget 30, 40, 51
 by-elections to 41, 153
 & Cabinet 22–3, 30–1, 40, 45, 50–5
 committees of 53–4
 conflict with Lords 13, 15, 39
 disqualifications 42, 56–7
 effective 55
 foreign counterparts 53

 Foreign Secretaries in 16
 Leader of 50–1
 & media 74, 76
 ministerial involvement 54
 need for majority in 18–19, 26–7, 30–2, 36, 40, 43–4, 93
 parties in 5, 30–2, 40, 52, 54–5, 99
 power of 15, 32, 39–40, 43–4, 51–5, 75
 & Prime Minister 17, 23, 26–7, 40, 43, 53–4
 procedure of 8, 51–5, 152
 prolonging life of 17, 39
 questions in 51, 53
 representative character of 40–4, 90
 Speaker of 37, 46, 51
 traditions 53–4
 & treaties 28–9
 & Ulster 131, 136
 vexing 51–5
 votes of confidence 30–1, 43, 51–5
 Whips 50, 52
House of Lords
 abolition 13, 38–9, 99, 104
 acts as supreme court 46
 & Cabinet 22, 45, 50
 defeating government 30, 39
 delaying power 15, 38–9, 76
 Foreign Secretaries in 16
 hereditary peers 16, 38
 life peers 38
 majority not essential in 39
 overcoming opposition of 13, 15, 38–9
 parties in 5
 presided by Lord Chancellor 46
 Prime Ministers in 17
 promotion to 32, 98
 televised 40
Hungary 133

India 79, 80, 83–4, 119, 138
Indonesia 121
International organisations (*see also* EEC, NATO)
 Council of Europe 105

International organisations –
  continued
  General Agreement on Tariffs &
    Trade (GATT) 107
  International Monetary Fund
    (IMF) 107, 110, 156
  United Nations 72, 83
Ireland (*see also* Ulster)
  civil war in 131, 137
  Commonwealth 80
  dominion 78
  history 129–34
  Home Rule 15, 87, 130
  Irish Republican Army (IRA)
    95, 133–7
  neutrality of 131
  politics in 131
  Prime Ministers of 129
  Republic of 18, 80, 112, 131
  trade unions in 67
Isle of Man 33
Israel 12, 119, 138
  Palestine Liberation Organisation
    (PLO) 95, 133
Italy 69, 85, 112, 121

Japan 82, 109, 112–14, 150
Justice
  European Court 105
  judges 29, 42, 46, 56–7, 64, 105,
    142, 144
  judiciary 22, 38, 45–6, 63–4, 104
  juries 17–18, 64
  justices of the peace 64
  legal aid 64, 105
  magistrates 56–7, 62, 64
  political trials 17

Kenya 86
King Edward VII (*b*. 1841 *s*. 1901
  d. 1910) 13, 34
King Edward VIII (*b*. 1894 *s*. 1936
  abdicated 1936 *d*. 1972) 34–5,
  74–5
King Ethelred II (*b*. 968 *s*. 978
  d.1016) 75
King George I (*b*. 1667 *s*. 1714
  d. 1727) 33, 99

King George V (*b*. 1865 *s*. 1910
  d. 1936) 13, 15, 34–5, 37, 62
King George VI (*b*. 1895 *s*. 1936
  d. 1952) 34
King James I and VI (*b*. 1566
  s. 1603 *d*. 1635) 33, 129
King James II (*b*. 1633 *s*. 1685
  deposed 1688 *d*. 1701) 158
King William III (*b*. 1651 *s*. 1689
  d. 1702) 153
King William IV (*b*. 1765 *s*. 1830
  d. 1837) 13, 33
Kinnock, Neil (1942–): British
  politician 6, 95, 119, 156
Kissinger, Henry (1923–): US
  Secretary of State 5, 122

Labour disputes 18, 68–71, 102,
  116, 153
  British record compared 69
  frequency 109
  & law 111
  & public opinion 144
  winter of discontent 110
Labour Party
  & bureaucracy 49, 65, 104
  choice of leader 16, 25, 31, 93
  composition 5, 88–9, 92, 94–5
  constitutional ideas 16, 25, 39,
    99, 101, 104, 107
  & defence 118, 122–3, 126–8,
    155, 157
  divisions in 18, 88, 90–1, 94–5,
    115, 117, 122
  & economy 88–9, 104, 106–7,
    114–17, 155–6
  & EEC 18, 24–5, 104, 106–7,
    111, 121–8
  electoral record 26, 36–7, 40–2,
    89–90, 92, 94, 109–11, 117
  emergency powers 29
  factions 88–90, 94–5, 117
  & foreign policy 118, 122–3
  ideology 89–90, 103–4, 115, 156
  leaders 6, 18, 26, 81, 89–90, 95,
    104, 119, 127, 156
  & local government 72, 95
  manifestos 20, 59, 90
  & media 74, 104

Labour Party – *continued*
  National Executive Committee 50
  nationalisation 90
  & overseas policy 120–8
  party chairman 50
  party conferences 18, 25, 31, 104, 127–8
  & peerages 98
  prospects of 13, 27, 92, 117, 127–8, 153, 155–6
  relies on trade union support 31, 67, 88, 97
  reselection of MPs 31, 90
  in Scotland 94
  Shadow Cabinet 25
  & trade unions 67–8, 88–91, 93, 109, 110–11, 115
  & Ulster 136–7
  & US 118, 122
  winter of discontent 110
Law
  adversary principle 64
  Church of England 75
  comparison with other countries 64, 74
  cost of 105
  immigration & nationality 84–6
  legal aid 105
  & media 74
Lebanon 133, 152–3
Left wing
  British 5, 60, 89, 94–6, 110, 125–8
  hard 94–5, 98, 107
  ideology 7, 64, 81, 139, 147
  in local government 95
  Militant Tendency 72, 95, 104
  moderate 94–5
  'no enemies on' 95
  peers 14, 39
  siege economy 110, 115
  soft 94–5
  swing to 117
  Trotskyists 95
Legitimacy in Britain 33–44, 65–6, 68–71
Lenin, V. I. (1870–1924): Soviet leader 2, 141

Liberal Party (British)
  composition 92
  constitutional ideas 16, 96
  & defence 126
  electoral record 36–7, 40–2, 91–2
  factions 96
  funds 97–8
  Gladstone 115, 148
  leader 16, 92–3
  & nuclear weapons 96
  overtaken by Labour 89
  proportional representation 91, 96
  splits 91
  supports Labour 91
  voters 92
Libya 12, 157
Lloyd George, David, later Earl (1863–1945): British Prime Minister 32, 48, 98, 100
Local government
  & central control 23, 50, 71–2, 101
  councillors and officials 58, 71–2
  finance 71–2
  housing 90
  left wing activities in 95
  & police 62
  rivals of State 66, 76, 95

MacDonald, Ramsay (1866–1937): British Prime Minister 31, 43, 48
Macmillan, Harold, later Lord Stockton (1894–1987): British Prime Minister 23, 45, 53, 93, 102, 113, 115
Malaya 83
Marxism 3, 89, 135
Media
  American 73
  British 66, 73–6, 104
  British Broadcasting Corporation (BBC) 62, 73–4
  & grievances 105, 116
  international comparison 74
Melbourne, Lord (1779–1848): British Prime Minister 46–7

Members of Parliament (MPs) (*see also* House of Commons)
  choice of candidates 98
  dependence on party support 31–2, 44, 52, 90
  election of 41–3, 57, 144
  facilities 53
  magistrates 57
  miscellaneous 1, 60
  & political consultants 105
  privileges 44, 54
  redress of grievances 105, 144
  women 143
Ministers (*see also* Prime Ministers)
  appointment 23, 25
  burden of voting 45–6
  Chancellor of the Exchequer 22, 111–12
  Chief Whip 50, 52
  dismissal of 15, 23–5
  duties of 122
  & House of Commons 54–5
  independence of 50, 54
  Lord Chancellor 22, 46, 56
  Lord President of the Council 22
  Lord Privy Seal 22
  miscellaneous 1, 22, 60, 105
  need for party support 31–2, 90
  & officials 58–62
  & Prime Ministers 23–7, 50
  private secretaries of 24, 50
  & Privy Council 29
  qualifications 22, 45
  & royal prerogative 28–9
  Secretaries of State 22, 61–2
  secrets kept from 24, 61
  titles 22
  & Whips 50
Monarchy
  advantages of 34–8
  British 8, 15, 17, 23, 29, 33–9, 75
  death warrant myth 64
  mystique of 37–8
Murray, Len (1922–): British trade unionist 69
Multinational corporations 66, 72–3, 76

Napoleon I (1769–1821): French Emperor 12, 64
Napoleon III (1808–73): French Emperor 102
National Health Service
  at Christmas 109
  deficiencies 116, 150, 154
  & parties 155
  Ulster 131
National Union of Mineworkers
  character 66
  & law 68, 70
  leadership 6, 70, 96
  strikes 63–4, 66, 68, 70–1, 75, 102, 116
  Union of Democratic Mineworkers 66
Netherlands 82, 112, 121, 124, 152
Newfoundland 78, 80
New Zealand 12, 78–80, 83–4
Nigeria 83
North Atlantic Treaty Organisation (NATO)
  British membership 110, 125–8
  nuclear strategy 126
North Sea Oil 19, 112, 115, 155
Nuclear weapons
  American in Britain 90, 96, 102, 126–8
  British 24, 47, 75, 90, 92, 96, 118, 127–8
  Campaign for Nuclear Disarmament (CND) 96, 126
  limited nuclear war 127
  political importance of 128, 156
  removal from British Isles 128, 157

Observer 11
Official Secrets Acts 17, 60–1, 74
Oman 12
Opposition 6, 37, 51–2, 54, 59, 97, 155
Orders in Council (*see also* Privy Council) 29–30, 52
Orwell, George (1903–50): British writer 5, 63

Owen, David (1938–): British politician 16, 44, 91–2
Oxford, University of 5–6, 116–17

Pakistan 80, 84, 119
Parliament (*see also* House of Commons, House of Lords)
 Acts of 29–30
 & Cabinet 23, 32, 50
 dissolution 15–17, 23, 29, 32, 36, 43–4
 European 53
 & foreign affairs 28–9
 hung 16
 & judges 56
 legislation 22, 51–5
Parliamentary Commissioner for Administration 105
 summoned 29
 threatened 102
Persian Gulf 83, 123
Pitt, William (1759–1806): British Prime Minister 17, 148
Playfair, Lyon, later Lord (1818–98): British prophet 151
Plebiscites 18–20, 92–3, 99, 123
Police (British)
 character & reputation 63, 65, 103, 141–2, 146
 control of 22, 62–3, 104
 organisation 62–3
 position in law 141–3
 Special Branch 62
 special constables 102
 & trade unions 69–70, 143
Political parties
 American 5, 7
 British 5–6, 15–16, 27, 30–2, 42, 50, 52, 59, 66, 87–98, 143
 choice of candidates 42, 90, 93, 98
 Christian Democrats 87
 euphemistic names 87
 factions 94–6, 98
 & magistrates 57
 miscellaneous 2
 unpopular 98
Politics
 academic subject viii, 101

business of Parliament 144
 definition 1
 & meteorology 148
 power over people 1–4, 6, 9, 20
 prediction in 148, 151
 systems 3, 7, 45–6, 49–50, 57–8, 90, 106
 writers on viii, 143, 147
Pollard, Professor Sidney (1925–): British writer 113
Pompidou, Georges (1911–1974): French President 122
Portugal 121
Powell, Enoch (1912–): British politician 44
Prime Ministers
 appointment of 26–7, 36, 93
 Asquith 13, 15, 37, 87
 Attlee 26, 47, 81, 97, 118
 Balfour 31
 Baldwin 17, 45, 98
 Callaghan 5–6, 19, 26–7, 43, 48, 52, 118
 Chamberlain 30–1, 52, 148
 choice of 15, 36, 93, 104
 Churchill 25–6, 31, 81, 98, 158
 & Conservative Party 50, 93
 Douglas-Home 6, 93
 Eden 26–7, 31, 118
 Gladstone 115, 148
 Grey 13–14, 17
 Heath 18, 36–7, 68, 70, 109, 122–4
 & House of Commons 32, 43–4, 54, 93
 international constraints on 10
 & Labour Party 24, 93, 104
 Lloyd George 32, 48, 98, 100
 MacDonald 31, 43, 48
 Macmillan 23, 27, 45, 53, 93, 102, 113
 Melbourne 46–7
 needs majority 26, 30–2
 needs party support 30–2
 not elected as such 26
 origin of office 99
 patronage of 23, 75
 peers supposedly ineligible 17
 Pitt 17, 148

Prime Ministers – *continued*
  political constraints on 25, 32
  power over Cabinet 23, 27, 32,
    43, 46–50, 54
  right to dissolution 37, 40–1, 43
  Thatcher 16, 24–6, 31, 37, 43–4,
    48, 53, 61, 68–74, 81, 101–3,
    111–18, 123–5, 127–8, 141,
    144, 151, 153–5, 158
  Wilson 18, 24–5, 27, 31, 36, 45,
    49, 68, 93, 108–9
  woman as 17, 144
Privy Council 29, 33
Public opinion 17–18, 63, 74–5, 83,
  103, 106, 111, 116–17
  polls 92, 96, 99–100, 113, 115,
    125, 127

Queen Anne (*b*. 1665 *s*. 1702
  d. 1714) 13–15, 33, 39
Queen Elizabeth I (*b*. 1534 *s*. 1558
  d. 1603) 35, 85, 141
Queen Elizabeth II (*b*. 1926
  s. 1952)
  acts on advice 27, 75, 80–1
  & ambassadors 27–8
  appoints Prime Ministers 26–7,
    36, 93
  & bishops 2
  commissions 27–8, 65
  & Commonwealth 77–82
  Defender of the Faith 77, 80
  descent 33
  Duke of Normandy 33
  international status 82
  popularity 34–5
  powers of 15–18, 26–8, 32–8
  Private Secretary 16, 81
  Queen's pleasure 56
  ratifies treaties 28–9
  refusal of dissolution 36–7
  rights of 36
  style and title 77, 80
  & Thatcher 81
Queen Victoria (*b*. 1819 *s*. 1837
  d. 1901) 28, 33–6, 102

Reagan, Ronald (1911–): US
  President 26, 117

Revolution
  American 8
  consequences 8
  contrasted with evolution 10, 106
  fear of 13, 87, 95, 102
  French 8, 17
  Glorious 153
  Russian 8, 156
Rhodesia 72, 86, 123
Right wing
  Fascists 142
  & foreign policy 126–7
  ideology 7, 94
  & Labour Party 90
  National Front 94
  & racialism 94
  radicals of 60, 104, 125
Roman Empire 2, 81, 85, 129, 152–3
Romania 4
Royal prerogative 13, 16, 28–9, 32,
  35, 93
Royalty 4, 34–6, 82
Royal veto 15, 39, 76

Saudi Arabia 4, 12
Scargill, Arthur (1938–): British
  trade unionist 6, 72, 102
Scotland
  elections in 42
  foreigners in 145
  history 129, 149, 157
  independence 19–20, 157
  Labour Party in 94
  legal system 49–50, 64
  media in 73
  plebiscite in 19
  Scottish National Party 19, 93–4,
    96
  Scots Against War 97
  Secretary of State for 62
  trade unions in 67
  Workers' Revolutionary Party 96
Second World War
  British options 157
  & conscription 62, 82, 118
  & decolonisation 78–9
  economic consequences 84, 108–9, 119, 150, 158

Second World War – *continued*
  lessons of 120
  political consequences 119, 126, 145
  prolongs House of Commons 17, 41
Singapore 120, 123
Skidelsky, Professor (1939–): British writer 112
Social Democratic Party (British)
  composition 92
  constitutional ideas 16
  & defence 126
  electoral record 42, 91–2
  funds 97
  leader 16, 91–3, 96
  & nuclear weapons 96
  origin 90–1
  proportional representation 91–2
  voters 92
Socialism
  in Britain 8, 64, 89–90, 95, 104, 121
  in Ireland 134–5
  in United States 8
  Young 95
South Africa 72, 78, 80–1, 83, 86, 123, 128, 144–5
Soviet Union
  British relations with 73, 89, 95, 119, 126
  Chernobyl accident 157
  & détente 126
  foreign policy of 82, 126
  governing class in 3–7
  law in 64, 142
  magnitude 150
  Nomenklatura 3, 7
  political evolution of 7, 148
  trade unions in 69
Spain 69, 112
Stalin, Josef (1879–1953): Soviet leader 6, 95, 126
State (British)
  & civil liberties 139–41, 143–7
  enemies of 87, 103
  foreign constraints on 106–7
  institutions of 17, 22–32, 38, 61, 98

  & law 64
  nature & purpose 100
  & parties 97–8
  rivals of 66–76, 87, 102–3, 145, 147
  servants of 56–65, 69, 145–7
  violent challenge to 70–1, 95–7, 102–3, 106–7, 140
  welfare 89, 94, 101, 104, 132
  wicked animal 103
Steel, David (1938–): British politician
  & Alliance 92
  constitutional ideas 16
  & Liberal Party 16, 92–3
Suez adventure of 1956 24, 83, 118, 121
Sunday Times 80–1
Sweden 66, 85, 98, 119, 149–50
Switzerland 85, 95, 98, 149–50, 152

Taverne, Dick (1928–): British politician 44
Thatcher, Margaret (1925–): British Prime Minister
  & Americans 158
  ascendancy over ministers 24–5
  best allies of 117
  & civil servants 61, 69
  & Commonwealth 83
  & Conservative Party 31, 94
  & defence 118, 123, 127–8
  & economy 71–2, 101, 111–17, 153
  & education 116–17, 151
  & foreign policy 72–3, 118, 123–5, 127–8
  future 37, 117, 153
  & House of Commons 53
  & liberty 74, 101, 141, 144
  & Oxford 116–17
  & peers 16, 39
  & plebiscites 18
  & Queen 80–1
  & State 101–3
  'uncaring' 116
Times, The 16, 31, 81, 116
Tocqueville, Alexis de (1805–59): French prophet 148
Toynbee, Arnold (1889–1975): British writer 152

Trade unions
  assistance to members 105
  & British politics 5, 45, 66–71, 76, 93–4, 96, 101
  claim to independence 69, 73
  Congress of 67, 69
  & Conservative Party 88, 101
  & immigration 145–6
  & Labour Party 67, 88–91, 93, 97, 109–11, 115
  largest 66
  & law 68–70
  Left in 96
  & media 75
  power of 76, 97, 111, 144–6, 152
  rights of members 93, 143
  & servants of the State 69, 143

Uganda 86
Ulster (Northern Ireland)
  administration of 50, 130–2, 135–7
  & British army 130–8
  & churches 75
  civil rights in 132, 135
  Curragh Mutiny (1914) 62
  disengagement 130, 137
  elections in 42, 44, 136
  foreign interference 87, 134–5
  history 129–33
  Irish Republican Army (IRA) 95, 133–7
  net cost of 137
  plebiscite in 18
  police in 62, 132–3, 135–6
  prime ministers of 132
  religion in 129–37
  resistance 87, 130, 136–7
  special problem of 129–38
  suicide in 109, 136
  terrorism in 74, 134–7
  trade unions in 67, 136
  violence in 132–7
United Kingdom 18, 33, 50, 64, 77, 80, 84
United States
  British relations with 35, 73, 96, 106, 118–23, 126–8, 158
  civil war 14, 20
  constitution of 12, 14, 27–8, 38, 42, 49, 51, 53–4, 58, 73, 75, 100
  crime in 102, 158
  & Diego Garcia 123
  disaffection in 106
  economy of 108, 112
  education 151
  governing class of 4–5, 7, 58, 65
  immigration 85
  judiciary 64
  media in 73–4
  & Philippines 81
  political evolution of 7–8, 79, 119, 141
  political parties in 5, 7, 87, 97–8
  presidents of 5, 7–8, 24–6, 51, 54, 58–60, 102, 117
  & Russia 148
  size of 150
  socialism in 8
  suicide in 109
  Supreme Court 15
  trade unions 66, 68–9
  & Ulster 132, 134–5
  & Vietnam 121–2
  Watergate Crisis 14

Wales
  chauvinism in 145
  elections in 42
  history 129
  independence 19
  language 94
  nationalist party 93–4, 97
  Plaid Cymru 94
  plebiscites in 19, 94
  suicide in 109
  trade unions in 67
Who, Whom? 2, 10, 141
Wilson, Harold, later Lord Wilson of Rievaulx (1916–): British Prime Minister 18–19, 24–5, 31, 36, 45, 49, 68, 89, 108–10, 118, 122, 148, 156
  Final Term 36
Wilson, Woodrow (1856–1924): US President 25–6
Women, rights of 15, 97, 140, 143–4

GPSR Compliance
The European Union's (EU) General Product Safety Regulation (GPSR) is a set of rules that requires consumer products to be safe and our obligations to ensure this.

If you have any concerns about our products, you can contact us on

ProductSafety@springernature.com

In case Publisher is established outside the EU, the EU authorized representative is:

Springer Nature Customer Service Center GmbH
Europaplatz 3
69115 Heidelberg, Germany

www.ingramcontent.com/pod-product-compliance
Ingram Content Group UK Ltd.
Pitfield, Milton Keynes, MK11 3LW, UK
UKHW041417180426
11947UKWH00007B/184